If found, kindly return to:

Name: _____

Phone: _____

Greatly appreciated

THE STRESS-LESS LIFE GUIDE

TEENS

The simplest and most effective steps to a happier, healthier, and successful life!

CREATED BY
Dr. DIANNA M. and GABRIELLA K.
The Mother and Daughter Team

On top of our current monthly donations, a percentage of sales from ALL of our books will support children with mental and other health issues, some YouTube channels, and animal shelters that are helping abused and homeless animals.

Printed in the United States of America

First Printing, 2018

ISBN 978-1-7322971-1-1

Stress-Less Way Publishing

Connect with us:

Email: team@stresslessway.com

www.stresslessway.com

WELCOME!

The Mother and Daughter Team would like YOU to join us on the exciting journey to a Stress-Less Life!

Presented for your attention is a series of Guides with daily Journals and Coloring Pages for **ALL ages.** They will provide you with a practical step-by-step tool to facilitate inner peace, reduce your daily stress and lead to a more productive life.

Only together, with the help of *parents, close family members, teachers, and medical professionals,* can we build a safer environment for us, our children, and future generations.

OTHER GUIDES IN THIS SERIES:

- THE STRESS-LESS LIFE GUIDE - ADULTS.
- THE STRESS-LESS LIFE GUIDE - SUMMERTIME OR ANYTIME - TEENS.
- THE STRESS-LESS LIFE GUIDE - KIDS AND PARENTS.
- THE STRESS-LESS LIFE GUIDE - SUMMERTIME OR ANYTIME - KIDS AND PARENTS.

ENJOY OUR:

NEWEST AND ONGOING SERIES OF INCREDIBLY INSPIRING **STRESS-LESS COLORING BOOKS** FOR DIFFERENT AGES.

These books include inspiring Quotes and Drawings from ACTUAL children and adults, some of whom have very challenging health issues.

Disclaimer

Presented below, The Stress-Less Life Guide was created for educational and learning purposes only. Our ultimate goal is to provide a useful aid for anyone, including parents, professionals, schoolteachers and doctors. It is never too late to be on the way to your own Stress-Less life. Integrating our practices and methods into your lives on a daily basis will allow you and your loved ones to cope with stress more intelligently. You will learn how to guide yourself to a more fulfilling and stressless life. You will be in charge of your health, happiness, and future success. By following these Guides, you will be inspired to share your newfound skills with many others along your path.

TABLE OF CONTENTS

FOREWORD

Hello fellow readers! It is a privilege to introduce you to the world of The Stress-Less Life Guides. My name is Dr. Anton Fisher, D.O. I am a licensed and Board Certified Psychiatrist. I was asked to review the contents of these books. Having done so, I wholeheartedly recommend them to readers of all ages.

Stress, which is Anxiety by another name, has always been difficult to treat. There are various known forms of psychotherapy recommended for stress, and they often involve journaling. This series of guides will help lead you on a path of self-discovery and understanding of the underlying factors of what is causing your stress. Completing the exercises in the journals will be an outlet for your negative emotions and help to deflate your stressors from your day. Some of these guides are meant for children or adolescents. Completing them together with a parent will help create or strengthen your family bond. The guides can also be completed on your own, with family, or in conjunction with a professional therapist.

I personally know the authors of these guides and the circumstances that led them to want to help our society at large. Their combined wisdom, experience, and unique perspectives helped create these journals.

This series of guides will introduce you to some of those rare books that can be a benefit to everyone. I am confident that following the exercises in these journals will lead to a reduction in anxiety/stress levels and improved functioning at work, school, home, and life in general.

Dr. Anton Fisher, D.O.

Dr. Anton Fisher, D.O. is a Board Certified Psychiatrist practicing in multiple states, including Nevada. He is the founder of **TeleMind™**, a novel telepsychiatry clinic located in the Las Vegas Valley and beyond. More information can be found at www.telemindclinic.com.

*Disclaimer: I do not have a financial interest in these guides. These guides are not a substitute for medical advice. If you believe you are experiencing symptoms of a mood, anxiety, attention or other disorder, please consult with a mental health professional. I waive any liability for the content or effects of these guides.

OUR STORY...

Hi there!

- My name is DIANNA.
- And my name is GABRIELLA.

We are The Mother and Daughter Team!

With the significant amount of unspeakable events happening around the world recently, we could not just sit back and wait for another tragedy to happen.

We decided to be proactive and take small, but essential steps, to create a better world for all of us and for future generations to come.

We believe that **only together** can we make a difference and help people we love and respect.

Our ultimate goal is to try to create a peaceful, safe, and positive environment with less stress and cruelty.

We are hoping that our Guides/Journals will provide an excellent aid for children and their families, for teachers and medical professionals, and for the general public at large.

Parents and grandparents will have an invaluable opportunity to bond more closely with their kids and grandkids. Siblings will strengthen their connections and hopefully will become more tolerant towards each other. By doing this project together, the families will develop a better understanding and respect for one another. This Guide will help to improve communication between families, schools and mental health professionals when needed.

We believe that by using the steps outlined below, you can change the way you react to stressful situations in your everyday life.

With all our efforts combined, we can create a less angry, less depressed, and a less self-absorbed society. Consequently, we will all live in a more safe and positive world.

LOVE AND PEACE

Dianna M.
Gabi K.

A MESSAGE FOR PARENTS...

(Teens can peek)

Hello from the Mother and Daughter Team!

What could be a better way to connect with and understand your child than by spending time together while discussing problems or successes? I don't consider phone calls, texts, and social media messages as an actual communication. Nothing will replace a real face-to-face interaction.

It is difficult to find time in our hectic lives. But, it is extremely important to establish this connection from an early age. Coming from my very own life lessons and experiences, I strongly believe it is much easier to recognize, correct, and prevent future behavioral and emotional problems at a young age.

I've been blessed with three healthy children and a beautiful grandson. Looking back, I can definitely say - I could've done a better job connecting with them. I regret not spending more time listening to their concerns when they were little. Unfortunately, I can't go back in time.

Having said that, we should learn valuable lessons from past mistakes. It is easy to criticize all the wrong turns that we took, but we have to understand that every one of those experiences was shaping us into who we are today. Those stressful events taught us how to be more compassionate to others and how to love ourselves along with the people who are important to us.

On a positive note:

Completing these Guides/Journals projects with my teenage daughter gave us so much joy. We really connected and bonded over thinking and brainstorming together. Seeing her take an interest in something that's important to me makes me feel like she genuinely cares about what I do with my life. And that's so special. While finishing these Guides together, I see she also developed a selfless drive to help her loved ones, her local community, and our society.

My daughter had a heart-breaking experience that personally drove us to publish these Guides. She has a few close friends who also deal with things like depression, stress, and anxiety. One of her friends, unfortunately, couldn't handle whatever was going on within himself and ended up taking his own life...

This is why this project is so important to the both of us. We are genuinely hoping it will guide parents and close family members to developing an understanding with their children.

We believe that learning how to manage stress at a young age can help shield our children from depression, anger, anxiety, and self-destructive habits later in their lives. Hopefully, it will protect them from potential outrageous behaviors that may lead to irreversible damages.

To create a better and safer environment for our future generations to come - we have to start guiding our children NOW.

We have to try to prevent potential future mishaps as much as we can. We hope this Guide will help you connect with your children like never before and serve the public good.

Reviewing this guide with your teenagers, as they need it, will reveal other stressors and secrets that affect their lives. You will discover intimate details of your child's life that would have remained hidden otherwise. You will unearth and subsequently have the ability to address your child's needs. You will discover your child's talents and interests; perhaps even prevent a future tragedy.

Encouraging our children with kindness and moral support is one of the best things we can do for them. That alone will be one of the greatest lessons for their future. While guiding our kids to happiness and success, we have to keep reminding them that hard work and determination pay off.

We also recommend you to engage in The Stress-Less Life Guide for ADULTS. This would help you master the techniques your child is learning yourself while reducing your own stress levels.

LOVE AND PEACE

Dianna M.
Gabi K.

MY STORY...

Hi there!

My name is Gabriella, and I am a curious adolescent with many thoughts and reflections on the typical stressful life of a teenager. I am sure that many of you can relate to this long-standing issue. Although some of this down below is going to be explained to you in general terms, most of it is from my own experiences.

It's not easy being a teen in today's world!

You have to deal with teenage hormones, which change your character even if you don't notice it. My family is always saying to me: "You've got it easy now. Your only responsibilities are school and occasional jobs." That may be true, but in our eyes, we live in a completely different world, with different rules. We are trying to survive in a world full of stress, pressure, and these crazy expectations that ideally should not exist in the first place. **A few examples...**

First, academic load. We have to worry about so many things and have to juggle multiple tasks at once - completing reports and projects, studying for exams, thinking about the future and college. *Don't get me wrong; I know that some stress is healthy and encourages me to perform better in school.* It is just so overwhelming at times. Most of this stress was distracting me from accomplishing my goals in their entirety.

Second, there is so much social pressure; it's unbelievable. If you don't act or look a certain way in someone else's eyes, you're shamed and judged. Consequently, I think teenagers often have to put aside their true self and pretend to be someone they are not, which can stress us out even more. Not to forget about occasional relationship problems with family, friends, boyfriends/girlfriends. It all adds up.

Luckily, I can control my emotions to some extent when it comes to things like that, but I still needed to learn how to manage stress better. Although, if you aren't that way, and things do tend to get to you, then you may begin to suffer both inside and out.

Some of the **emotional side effects** we get to experience out of this are anger, anxiety, depression, mood swings, irritability, panic attacks, etc.

A few of the **physical signs** include: tiredness, headaches, nausea, loss or increase of appetite, and, sometimes, losing interest in pursuing your hobbies or extracurricular activities.

Just have to mention **a few more potential problems** that may lead to more stress:
- Financial difficulties
- Traumatic events: death, abuse, bullying, health problems
- Moving and changing schools
- Dealing with additions to the family: sibling and/or stepparents
- Peer pressure and poor self-esteem
- Constant distractions by technology and media lead to poor time management, negativity, decreasing of actual human interaction, and not our best performance in school. It feels like we never have time for anything.

The list is endless...

BUT!!!! ON THE **POSITIVE NOTE**, COMING COMPLETELY FROM OUR OWN EXPERIENCES, MY MOM AND I WILL TRY TO HELP YOU TO MINIMIZE YOUR STRESS AND WORRIES AS MUCH AS POSSIBLE!

Practicing in this Journal has benefited me in ways I would have never imagined. It serves as my **"security blanket"**. Whenever I feel something is out of my control or something I can't handle, I turn to this Journal, and I write whatever is on my mind. After writing in it daily, I can better understand that most of my problems and worries were actually baseless.

Whatever was a "big" issue yesterday turned out to be not a big deal at all a couple of days later! **Most** of my problems were solved one way or another, or forgotten. **Some** of them were out of my control to start with, so why bother?! I was stressing out for absolutely no reason.

As it has done for me, I firmly believe this Guide will prepare you to be in control of your future hardships and life in general.
My mom and I definitely got better with our stress management. I am starting college this coming fall, and the acquired knowledge and habits are priceless. I will try my best to apply them all during my college years to reduce my expected stress and anxiety. I always keep my Guide close to me. It makes me feel more secure with all the life lessons and wisdom in it (my own experiences and

from others). I wish I could have started this Guide earlier in life. **But** it is never too late!

P.S. You will learn how to be in control of your own emotions and life at any age. Isn't that incredible?!

You still will be responsible for all the work, but don't worry. We'll do it together!

The Stress-Less Life Guide will get you, **step-by-step**, to a happier, more successful, and healthier lifestyle.
Daily practice will help you to form **new habits** that will lead you to a more stable future with less stress in it.

P.S. *To make it even more interesting, we also created a separate Stress-Less Life Guide that you can practice in during school breaks and holidays!*

JOIN US ON OUR LIFELONG JOURNEY TO YOUR HAPPINESS, HEALTH, AND SUCCESS!!!

WHAT TO EXPECT

How this Guide will help manage/control your daily stress:

1. With daily practice, you will learn how to switch your thoughts from negative to positive in a matter of seconds. The saying "practice makes perfect" never gets old. It creates a simple habit that you will benefit from in your day-to-day life.
2. On worry-free days (fantastic!) you can write about positive events only. It would be nice to be able to go back in time and rehash those precious moments in the future.
3. Yes, YOU will have to be willing to step out of your comfort zone and still do all the work in the real world. No magic there. But remember, you always have those few precious seconds to switch to positive thoughts.
4. It is important to do that switch fast. Our mind has a mind of its own and will try hard to trick us into something less pleasant if we're too slow. I'm sharing this from my personal experience.
5. Daily practice in this Journal will help you to react and behave intelligently during difficult situations.
6. You will see that your "BIG" problem was not actually as big as time passes. You will understand how truly insignificant the "problem" was. Your stress will be history, but **part of your health and happiness had been permanently stolen at that moment.**
7. "Time Heals"... The beauty of this Journal is that you can always go back and see for yourself that all those worries were groundless, and most of your problems are probably solved by now.
8. With time, you will gain better control over different situations and your mindful behavior.

9. You will be able to handle your future problems with ease and minimized stress.

You will eventually understand that most of these problems are temporary and will be resolved one way or another.
Remember - "Tomorrow is a better day."

The benefits that you will get using this Guide:

- You will be a happier and healthier person who will bring more positivity to the universe.
- You can share this knowledge with people you love, respect, and trust. You can teach them how to manage their stress. Consequently, you will be surrounded by positive people and become a part of a happy environment - "happy bubble" - a win-win situation.
- You will create an incredible bond with your family and people you value.
- You will concentrate on who and what is actually important in your life.
- You will perform your daily tasks more efficiently, with a full understanding that almost everything will be resolved sooner or later.
- You will be well conditioned against future mishaps.

Life is too short to waste your time with stress and worries.

LOVE AND PEACE

PRACTICE MAKES PERFECT

Steps to take daily or as needed:

The moment you feel stressed out or upset about something - **STOP:** BECOME MINDFUL AND AWARE. *Try to do the following:*

1. Limit your social media time to the minimum. Try to have a real face-to-face conversation with people you love and trust. Always remember YOU ARE NEVER ALONE with your problems and concerns! There is always someone around you who can help and guide you to proper solutions.

2. Tell yourself: "Tomorrow will be a better day, and my stress will be history. I am a healthy and happy individual." Even if you don't feel that way at that particular moment, make it as your mantra/affirmation. Repeat it as many times as needed to clear your mind from any negativity. Try to do it out loud if possible. That alone is a great way to start thinking positive thoughts.

3. Go to that positive place in your mind when you're stressed. Put as many happy thoughts and pictures as you want in that space and use them as needed. You can create your own inspirational quotes or use the ones from our Journal. You don't need many. *They have to be strong enough to serve as the switch from negative to positive.* That will be your own way out from your "stress bubble."

4. **Do what makes YOU happy:**
   - Listen to your favorite music.
   - Play your favorite instrument.
   - Spend time with positive people.
   - Read the books you love.
   - Watch a funny movie or video.
   - Just go outside for fresh air.
   - Draw/Color.
   - Go to the Gym.

There is *no end* to fun stuff that you can do to direct your mind toward positive thinking.

5. On a daily basis, at your convenience - ideally, right before night time - write in this Journal the reason/reasons why you were stressed and what made your day better. *Share your thoughts with your family to get proper guidance and great ideas.*

IF NOTHING MADE YOU UPSET - **FANTASTIC!!!**
CONTINUE ENJOYING YOUR DAY AND WRITE DOWN ONLY WHAT MADE YOU HAPPY TODAY.

6. Give it some time (however much is needed - a day/two days/a week) and revisit that page later.

You will be in shock. Most of those problems you will not even remember. **Some** of those problems were out of your control to begin with, so why bother? **The rest** of them were solved one way or another, as always. Stressing out was for absolutely **NOTHING!!!**

THAT IS IT!!!

A simple and effective way to control your emotions and stress levels. It works for us every time. I am sure it will work for you as well.

BY BEING A MASTER OF YOUR OWN MIND, THOUGHTS, AND BEHAVIOR, **YOU AND ONLY YOU** WERE ABLE TO TURN A STRESSFUL DAY INTO A HAPPY DAY!

P.S. IN THE FUTURE, THESE GUIDES WILL BECOME PRICELESS MEMORIES AND LIFE LESSONS FOR YOU AND YOUR OWN CHILDREN - SAVE THEM!

LOVE AND PEACE

THE MOTHER AND DAUGHTER TEAM

DAILY JOURNAL

I AM SO THANKFUL AND READY FOR AN AMAZING NEW DAY.
CAN'T WAIT TO SEE WHAT IT WILL BRING TODAY!

"Do not dwell in the past, do not dream of the future, concentrate the mind on the present moment."(1)
~Buddha

Date ___/___/20__

STRESSFUL MOMENTS:

_____

_____

_____

HAPPY MOMENTS:

_____

_____

_____

PLAN AHEAD TODAY TO MINIMIZE YOUR STRESS TOMORROW.
(OR YOU CAN JUST WRITE OR DRAW SOMETHING SILLY DOWN BELOW AND GO TO BED SMILING.)
PLANS FOR TOMORROW/TO DO LIST:

CREATE YOUR **OWN** INSPIRING **QUOTE** AND **SHARE YOUR WISDOM** WITH OTHERS!

_____

_____

Date ____/____/20____

STRESSFUL MOMENTS:

_____

_____

HAPPY MOMENTS:

_____

_____

Family Bonding Time...

-WRITE OR DRAW SOMETHING SILLY IN THE SPACE DOWN BELOW THAT WILL PUT A HUGE SMILE ON YOUR FACE. ALWAYS TRY TO GO TO BED SMILING AND FEELING HAPPY!

-THINK OF WAYS YOU CAN MAKE YOUR DAY EVEN BETTER TOMORROW.

-ALWAYS SHARE YOUR THOUGHTS AND CONCERNS (even when it is hard to do sometimes) WITH YOUR LOVING FAMILY FOR PROPER GUIDANCE AND GREAT IDEAS. WRITE THEM DOWN BELOW IF NEEDED.

Leaving a toxic place and toxic people are the best things that you can do for your peace of mind. Just be a bigger person and end the drama.

Date ___/___/20__

STRESSFUL MOMENTS:

_____

_____

_____

HAPPY MOMENTS:

_____

_____

_____

PLAN AHEAD TODAY TO MINIMIZE YOUR STRESS TOMORROW.
(OR YOU CAN JUST WRITE OR DRAW SOMETHING SILLY DOWN BELOW AND GO TO BED SMILING.)
PLANS FOR TOMORROW/TO DO LIST:

CREATE YOUR OWN INSPIRING QUOTE AND SHARE YOUR WISDOM WITH OTHERS!

_____

_____

Date ___/___/20__

STRESSFUL MOMENTS:

_____

_____

HAPPY MOMENTS:

_____

_____

_____

Family Bonding Time…

-WRITE OR DRAW SOMETHING SILLY IN THE SPACE DOWN BELOW THAT WILL PUT A HUGE SMILE ON YOUR FACE. ALWAYS TRY TO GO TO BED SMILING AND FEELING HAPPY!

-THINK OF WAYS YOU CAN MAKE YOUR DAY EVEN BETTER TOMORROW.

-ALWAYS SHARE YOUR THOUGHTS AND CONCERNS (even when it is hard to do sometimes) WITH YOUR LOVING FAMILY FOR PROPER GUIDANCE AND GREAT IDEAS. WRITE THEM DOWN BELOW IF NEEDED.

"If you believe in what you are doing, then let nothing hold you up in your work. Much of the best work of the world has been done against seeming impossibilities. The thing is to get the work done."(1)   ~Dale Carnegie

Date ___/___/20__

STRESSFUL MOMENTS:

_____

_____

_____

HAPPY MOMENTS:

_____

_____

_____

PLAN AHEAD TODAY TO MINIMIZE YOUR STRESS TOMORROW.
(OR YOU CAN JUST WRITE OR DRAW SOMETHING SILLY DOWN BELOW AND GO TO BED SMILING.)
PLANS FOR TOMORROW/TO DO LIST:

CREATE YOUR **OWN** INSPIRING **QUOTE** AND **SHARE YOUR WISDOM** WITH OTHERS!

_____

_____

Date ___/___/20__

STRESSFUL MOMENTS:

_____

_____

HAPPY MOMENTS:

_____

_____

_____

Family Bonding Time...

-WRITE OR DRAW SOMETHING SILLY IN THE SPACE DOWN BELOW THAT WILL PUT A HUGE SMILE ON YOUR FACE. ALWAYS TRY TO GO TO BED SMILING AND FEELING HAPPY!

-THINK OF WAYS YOU CAN MAKE YOUR DAY EVEN BETTER TOMORROW.

-ALWAYS SHARE YOUR THOUGHTS AND CONCERNS (even when it is hard to do sometimes) WITH YOUR LOVING FAMILY FOR PROPER GUIDANCE AND GREAT IDEAS. WRITE THEM DOWN BELOW IF NEEDED.

"Never sacrifice your class to get even with someone who has none. Let them have the gutter. You take the high road."(2)   ~unknown

Date ___/___/20__

STRESSFUL MOMENTS:

_____

_____

_____

HAPPY MOMENTS:

_____

_____

_____

PLAN AHEAD TODAY TO MINIMIZE YOUR STRESS TOMORROW.
(OR YOU CAN JUST WRITE OR DRAW SOMETHING SILLY DOWN BELOW AND GO TO BED SMILING.)
PLANS FOR TOMORROW/TO DO LIST:

CREATE your **OWN** inspiring **QUOTE** and **SHARE YOUR WISDOM WITH OTHERS!**

_____

_____

Date ___/___/20__

STRESSFUL MOMENTS:

_____

_____

HAPPY MOMENTS:

_____

_____

_____

Family Bonding Time...

-WRITE OR DRAW SOMETHING SILLY IN THE SPACE DOWN BELOW THAT WILL PUT A HUGE SMILE ON YOUR FACE. ALWAYS TRY TO GO TO BED SMILING AND FEELING HAPPY!

-THINK OF WAYS YOU CAN MAKE YOUR DAY EVEN BETTER TOMORROW.

-ALWAYS SHARE YOUR THOUGHTS AND CONCERNS (even when it is hard to do sometimes) WITH YOUR LOVING FAMILY FOR PROPER GUIDANCE AND GREAT IDEAS. WRITE THEM DOWN BELOW IF NEEDED.

"Life isn't about finding yourself. Life is about creating yourself."(1)

~Bernard Shaw

Date ___/___/20__

STRESSFUL MOMENTS:

_____

_____

_____

HAPPY MOMENTS:

_____

_____

_____

PLAN AHEAD TODAY TO MINIMIZE YOUR STRESS TOMORROW.
(OR YOU CAN JUST WRITE OR DRAW SOMETHING SILLY DOWN BELOW AND GO TO BED SMILING.)

PLANS FOR TOMORROW/TO DO LIST:

CREATE YOUR **OWN** INSPIRING **QUOTE** AND **SHARE YOUR WISDOM** WITH OTHERS!

_____

_____

Date ___ / ___ /20 __

STRESSFUL MOMENTS:

_____

_____

HAPPY MOMENTS:

_____

_____

_____

Family Bonding Time...

-WRITE OR DRAW SOMETHING SILLY IN THE SPACE DOWN BELOW THAT WILL PUT A HUGE SMILE ON YOUR FACE. ALWAYS TRY TO GO TO BED SMILING AND FEELING HAPPY!

-THINK OF WAYS YOU CAN MAKE YOUR DAY EVEN BETTER TOMORROW.

-ALWAYS SHARE YOUR THOUGHTS AND CONCERNS (even when it is hard to do sometimes) WITH YOUR LOVING FAMILY FOR PROPER GUIDANCE AND GREAT IDEAS. WRITE THEM DOWN BELOW IF NEEDED.

"Keep away from people who try to belittle your ambitions. Small people always do that, but the really great make you feel that you, too, can become great."[1]

~Mark Twain

Date ___ / ___ /20___

STRESSFUL MOMENTS:

_____

_____

_____

HAPPY MOMENTS:

_____

_____

_____

PLAN AHEAD TODAY TO MINIMIZE YOUR STRESS TOMORROW.
(OR YOU CAN JUST WRITE OR DRAW SOMETHING SILLY DOWN BELOW AND GO TO BED SMILING.)
PLANS FOR TOMORROW/TO DO LIST:

Don't judge others - so YOU will not be judged.

Date ___/___/20__

STRESSFUL MOMENTS:

_____

_____

_____

HAPPY MOMENTS:

_____

_____

_____

PLAN AHEAD TODAY TO MINIMIZE YOUR STRESS TOMORROW.
(OR YOU CAN JUST WRITE OR DRAW SOMETHING SILLY DOWN BELOW AND GO TO BED SMILING.)
PLANS FOR TOMORROW/TO DO LIST:

CREATE YOUR **OWN** INSPIRING **QUOTE** AND **SHARE YOUR WISDOM** WITH OTHERS!

_____

_____

Date ___/___/20__

STRESSFUL MOMENTS:

_____

_____

HAPPY MOMENTS:

_____

_____

Family Bonding Time...

-WRITE OR DRAW SOMETHING SILLY IN THE SPACE DOWN BELOW THAT WILL PUT A HUGE SMILE ON YOUR FACE. ALWAYS TRY TO GO TO BED SMILING AND FEELING HAPPY!
-THINK OF WAYS YOU CAN MAKE YOUR DAY EVEN BETTER TOMORROW.
-ALWAYS SHARE YOUR THOUGHTS AND CONCERNS (even when it is hard to do sometimes) WITH YOUR LOVING FAMILY FOR PROPER GUIDANCE AND GREAT IDEAS. WRITE THEM DOWN BELOW IF NEEDED.

"Progress is impossible without change, and those who cannot change their minds cannot change anything."[1]

~Bernard Shaw

Date ___ / ___ /20___

STRESSFUL MOMENTS:

_____

_____

_____

HAPPY MOMENTS:

_____

_____

_____

PLAN AHEAD TODAY TO MINIMIZE YOUR STRESS TOMORROW.

(OR YOU CAN JUST WRITE OR DRAW SOMETHING SILLY DOWN BELOW AND GO TO BED SMILING.)

PLANS FOR TOMORROW/TO DO LIST:

CREATE YOUR **OWN** INSPIRING **QUOTE** AND **SHARE YOUR WISDOM**
WITH OTHERS!

_____

_____

Date ___ / ___ /20 __

STRESSFUL MOMENTS:

_____

_____

HAPPY MOMENTS:

_____

_____

_____

Family Bonding Time...

-**WRITE OR DRAW SOMETHING SILLY IN THE SPACE DOWN BELOW THAT** WILL PUT A HUGE SMILE ON YOUR FACE. ALWAYS TRY TO GO TO BED SMILING AND FEELING HAPPY!
-**THINK** OF WAYS YOU CAN MAKE YOUR DAY EVEN BETTER TOMORROW.
-**ALWAYS SHARE** YOUR THOUGHTS AND CONCERNS (even when it is hard to do sometimes) WITH YOUR LOVING FAMILY FOR PROPER GUIDANCE AND GREAT IDEAS. WRITE THEM DOWN BELOW IF NEEDED.

"Success does not consist in never making mistakes but in never making the same one a second time."[1]

~Bernard Shaw

Date ___/___/20__

STRESSFUL MOMENTS:

_____

_____

_____

HAPPY MOMENTS:

_____

_____

_____

PLAN AHEAD TODAY TO MINIMIZE YOUR STRESS TOMORROW.

(OR YOU CAN JUST WRITE OR DRAW SOMETHING SILLY DOWN BELOW AND GO TO BED SMILING.)

PLANS FOR TOMORROW/TO DO LIST:

CREATE YOUR **OWN** INSPIRING **QUOTE** AND **SHARE YOUR WISDOM** WITH OTHERS!

_____

_____

Date ___/___/20__

STRESSFUL MOMENTS:

_____

_____

HAPPY MOMENTS:

_____

_____

Family Bonding Time...

-WRITE OR DRAW SOMETHING SILLY IN THE SPACE DOWN BELOW THAT WILL PUT A HUGE SMILE ON YOUR FACE. ALWAYS TRY TO GO TO BED SMILING AND FEELING HAPPY!

-THINK OF WAYS YOU CAN MAKE YOUR DAY EVEN BETTER TOMORROW.

-ALWAYS SHARE YOUR THOUGHTS AND CONCERNS (even when it is hard to do sometimes) WITH YOUR LOVING FAMILY FOR PROPER GUIDANCE AND GREAT IDEAS. WRITE THEM DOWN BELOW IF NEEDED.

"When people hurt you over and over, think of them like *sandpaper*. They may scratch and hurt a bit, but in the end, you end up *polished* and they end up *useless*."(2)   ~Anonymous

Date ___/___/20__

STRESSFUL MOMENTS:

_____

_____

_____

HAPPY MOMENTS:

_____

_____

_____

PLAN AHEAD TODAY TO MINIMIZE YOUR STRESS TOMORROW.
(OR YOU CAN JUST WRITE OR DRAW SOMETHING SILLY DOWN BELOW AND GO TO BED SMILING.)
PLANS FOR TOMORROW/TO DO LIST:

CREATE YOUR OWN INSPIRING QUOTE AND SHARE YOUR WISDOM WITH OTHERS!

_____

_____

Date ___/___/20__

STRESSFUL MOMENTS:

_____

_____

HAPPY MOMENTS:

_____

_____

_____

Family Bonding Time...

-WRITE OR DRAW SOMETHING SILLY IN THE SPACE DOWN BELOW THAT WILL PUT A HUGE SMILE ON YOUR FACE. ALWAYS TRY TO GO TO BED SMILING AND FEELING HAPPY!

-THINK OF WAYS YOU CAN MAKE YOUR DAY EVEN BETTER TOMORROW.

-ALWAYS SHARE YOUR THOUGHTS AND CONCERNS (even when it is hard to do sometimes) WITH YOUR LOVING FAMILY FOR PROPER GUIDANCE AND GREAT IDEAS. WRITE THEM DOWN BELOW IF NEEDED.

"A life spent making mistakes is not only more honorable, but more useful than a life spent doing nothing."(1)

~Bernard Shaw

Date ___/___/20__

STRESSFUL MOMENTS:

_____

_____

_____

HAPPY MOMENTS:

_____

_____

_____

PLAN AHEAD TODAY TO MINIMIZE YOUR STRESS TOMORROW.
(OR YOU CAN JUST WRITE OR DRAW SOMETHING SILLY DOWN BELOW AND GO TO BED SMILING.)
PLANS FOR TOMORROW/TO DO LIST:

CREATE YOUR **OWN** INSPIRING **QUOTE** AND **SHARE YOUR WISDOM WITH OTHERS!**

_____

_____

Date ___/___/20__

STRESSFUL MOMENTS:

_____

_____

HAPPY MOMENTS:

_____

_____

_____

Family Bonding Time...

-WRITE OR DRAW SOMETHING SILLY IN THE SPACE DOWN BELOW THAT WILL PUT A HUGE SMILE ON YOUR FACE. ALWAYS TRY TO GO TO BED SMILING AND FEELING HAPPY!

-THINK OF WAYS YOU CAN MAKE YOUR DAY EVEN BETTER TOMORROW.

-ALWAYS SHARE YOUR THOUGHTS AND CONCERNS (even when it is hard to do sometimes) WITH YOUR LOVING FAMILY FOR PROPER GUIDANCE AND GREAT IDEAS. WRITE THEM DOWN BELOW IF NEEDED.

"Very little is needed to make a happy life; it is all within yourself, in your way of thinking."(1)

~Marcus Aurelius

Date ___/___/20__

STRESSFUL MOMENTS:

_____

_____

_____

HAPPY MOMENTS:

_____

_____

_____

PLAN AHEAD TODAY TO MINIMIZE YOUR STRESS TOMORROW.

(OR YOU CAN JUST WRITE OR DRAW SOMETHING SILLY DOWN BELOW AND GO TO BED SMILING.)

PLANS FOR TOMORROW/TO DO LIST:

CREATE YOUR **OWN** INSPIRING **QUOTE** AND **SHARE YOUR WISDOM** WITH OTHERS!

_____

_____

Date ____/____/20____

STRESSFUL MOMENTS:

_____

_____

HAPPY MOMENTS:

_____

_____

_____

Family Bonding Time...

-WRITE OR DRAW SOMETHING SILLY IN THE SPACE DOWN BELOW THAT WILL PUT A HUGE SMILE ON YOUR FACE. ALWAYS TRY TO GO TO BED SMILING AND FEELING HAPPY!

-THINK OF WAYS YOU CAN MAKE YOUR DAY EVEN BETTER TOMORROW.

-ALWAYS SHARE YOUR THOUGHTS AND CONCERNS (even when it is hard to do sometimes) WITH YOUR LOVING FAMILY FOR PROPER GUIDANCE AND GREAT IDEAS. WRITE THEM DOWN BELOW IF NEEDED.

"Sometimes the best thing you can do is not think, not wonder, not imagine, not obsess. Just breathe and have faith that everything will work out for the best."(2)

~unknown

Date ___/___/20__

STRESSFUL MOMENTS:

_____

_____

_____

HAPPY MOMENTS:

_____

_____

_____

PLAN AHEAD TODAY TO MINIMIZE YOUR STRESS TOMORROW.

(OR YOU CAN JUST WRITE OR DRAW SOMETHING SILLY DOWN BELOW AND GO TO BED SMILING.)

PLANS FOR TOMORROW/TO DO LIST:

CREATE YOUR **OWN** INSPIRING **QUOTE** AND **SHARE YOUR WISDOM WITH OTHERS!**

_____

_____

Date ___/___/20__

STRESSFUL MOMENTS:

_____

_____

HAPPY MOMENTS:

_____

_____

Family Bonding Time...

-WRITE OR DRAW SOMETHING SILLY IN THE SPACE DOWN BELOW THAT WILL PUT A HUGE SMILE ON YOUR FACE. ALWAYS TRY TO GO TO BED SMILING AND FEELING HAPPY!

-THINK OF WAYS YOU CAN MAKE YOUR DAY EVEN BETTER TOMORROW.

-ALWAYS SHARE YOUR THOUGHTS AND CONCERNS (even when it is hard to do sometimes) WITH YOUR LOVING FAMILY FOR PROPER GUIDANCE AND GREAT IDEAS.

WRITE THEM DOWN BELOW IF NEEDED.

"The word 'happy' would lose its meaning if it were not balanced by sadness."[1]

~Carl Jung

Date ___/___/20__

STRESSFUL MOMENTS:

_____

_____

_____

HAPPY MOMENTS:

_____

_____

_____

PLAN AHEAD TODAY TO MINIMIZE YOUR STRESS TOMORROW.
(OR YOU CAN JUST WRITE OR DRAW SOMETHING SILLY DOWN BELOW AND GO TO BED SMILING.)
PLANS FOR TOMORROW/TO DO LIST:

It is Ok to love Yourself

"When you arise in the morning, think of what a precious privilege it is to be alive - to breathe, to think, to enjoy, to love."(1)   ~Marcus Aurelius

Date ___/___/20__

STRESSFUL MOMENTS:

_____

_____

_____

HAPPY MOMENTS:

_____

_____

_____

PLAN AHEAD TODAY TO MINIMIZE YOUR STRESS TOMORROW.
(OR YOU CAN JUST WRITE OR DRAW SOMETHING SILLY DOWN BELOW AND GO TO BED SMILING.)
PLANS FOR TOMORROW/TO DO LIST:

CREATE YOUR **OWN** INSPIRING **QUOTE** AND **SHARE YOUR WISDOM** WITH OTHERS!

_____

_____

Date ___/___/20__

STRESSFUL MOMENTS:

_____

_____

HAPPY MOMENTS:

_____

_____

Family Bonding Time...

-WRITE OR DRAW SOMETHING SILLY IN THE SPACE DOWN BELOW THAT WILL PUT A HUGE SMILE ON YOUR FACE. ALWAYS TRY TO GO TO BED SMILING AND FEELING HAPPY!

-**THINK** OF WAYS YOU CAN MAKE YOUR DAY EVEN BETTER TOMORROW.

-**ALWAYS SHARE** YOUR THOUGHTS AND CONCERNS (even when it is hard to do sometimes) WITH YOUR LOVING FAMILY FOR PROPER GUIDANCE AND GREAT IDEAS.

WRITE THEM DOWN BELOW IF NEEDED.

A negative mind will never give you a positive life. Stay positive. Just smile!

Date ___/___/20__

STRESSFUL MOMENTS:

_____

_____

_____

HAPPY MOMENTS:

_____

_____

_____

PLAN AHEAD TODAY TO MINIMIZE YOUR STRESS TOMORROW.
(OR YOU CAN JUST WRITE OR DRAW SOMETHING SILLY DOWN BELOW AND GO TO BED SMILING.)
PLANS FOR TOMORROW/TO DO LIST:

CREATE YOUR **OWN** INSPIRING **QUOTE** AND **SHARE YOUR WISDOM** WITH OTHERS!

_____

_____

Date ___/___/20___

STRESSFUL MOMENTS:

_____

_____

HAPPY MOMENTS:

_____

_____

_____

Family Bonding Time...

-**WRITE OR DRAW SOMETHING SILLY IN THE SPACE DOWN BELOW THAT** WILL PUT A HUGE SMILE ON YOUR FACE. ALWAYS TRY TO GO TO BED SMILING AND FEELING HAPPY!
-**THINK** OF WAYS YOU CAN MAKE YOUR DAY EVEN BETTER TOMORROW.
-**ALWAYS SHARE** YOUR THOUGHTS AND CONCERNS (even when it is hard to do sometimes) WITH YOUR LOVING FAMILY FOR PROPER GUIDANCE AND GREAT IDEAS. WRITE THEM DOWN BELOW IF NEEDED.

"You have power over your mind - not outside events. Realize this, and you will find strength."(1)

~Marcus Aurelius

Date ___/___/20__

STRESSFUL MOMENTS:

_____

_____

_____

HAPPY MOMENTS:

_____

_____

_____

PLAN AHEAD TODAY TO MINIMIZE YOUR STRESS TOMORROW.
(OR YOU CAN JUST WRITE OR DRAW SOMETHING SILLY DOWN BELOW AND GO TO BED SMILING.)
PLANS FOR TOMORROW/TO DO LIST:

CREATE YOUR OWN INSPIRING QUOTE AND SHARE YOUR WISDOM WITH OTHERS!

_____

_____

Date ___/___/20__

STRESSFUL MOMENTS:

_____

_____

HAPPY MOMENTS:

_____

_____

_____

Family Bonding Time...

-WRITE OR DRAW SOMETHING SILLY IN THE SPACE DOWN BELOW THAT WILL PUT A HUGE SMILE ON YOUR FACE. ALWAYS TRY TO GO TO BED SMILING AND FEELING HAPPY!

-THINK OF WAYS YOU CAN MAKE YOUR DAY EVEN BETTER TOMORROW.

-ALWAYS SHARE YOUR THOUGHTS AND CONCERNS (even when it is hard to do sometimes) WITH YOUR LOVING FAMILY FOR PROPER GUIDANCE AND GREAT IDEAS.

WRITE THEM DOWN BELOW IF NEEDED.

"Good habits formed at youth make all the difference."(1) ~Aristotle

Date ___/___/20__

STRESSFUL MOMENTS:

_____

_____

_____

HAPPY MOMENTS:

_____

_____

_____

PLAN AHEAD TODAY TO MINIMIZE YOUR STRESS TOMORROW.
(OR YOU CAN JUST WRITE OR DRAW SOMETHING SILLY DOWN BELOW AND GO TO BED SMILING.)
PLANS FOR TOMORROW/TO DO LIST:

CREATE YOUR OWN INSPIRING QUOTE AND SHARE YOUR WISDOM WITH OTHERS!

_____

_____

Date ___/___/20__

STRESSFUL MOMENTS:

_____

_____

HAPPY MOMENTS:

_____

_____

Family Bonding Time...

-WRITE OR DRAW SOMETHING SILLY IN THE SPACE DOWN BELOW THAT WILL PUT A HUGE SMILE ON YOUR FACE. ALWAYS TRY TO GO TO BED SMILING AND FEELING HAPPY!

-THINK OF WAYS YOU CAN MAKE YOUR DAY EVEN BETTER TOMORROW.

-ALWAYS SHARE YOUR THOUGHTS AND CONCERNS (even when it is hard to do sometimes) WITH YOUR LOVING FAMILY FOR PROPER GUIDANCE AND GREAT IDEAS.

WRITE THEM DOWN BELOW IF NEEDED.

"Everything in life is temporary. So if things are going good, enjoy it because it won't last forever. And if things are going bad, don't worry. It can't last forever either."(2)

~unknown

Date ___/___/20__

STRESSFUL MOMENTS:

_____

_____

_____

HAPPY MOMENTS:

_____

_____

_____

PLAN AHEAD TODAY TO MINIMIZE YOUR STRESS TOMORROW.

(OR YOU CAN JUST WRITE OR DRAW SOMETHING SILLY DOWN BELOW AND GO TO BED SMILING.)

PLANS FOR TOMORROW/TO DO LIST:

CREATE YOUR OWN INSPIRING QUOTE AND SHARE YOUR WISDOM WITH OTHERS!

_____

_____

Date ___/___/20__

STRESSFUL MOMENTS:

_____

_____

HAPPY MOMENTS:

_____

_____

Family Bonding Time...

-WRITE OR DRAW SOMETHING SILLY IN THE SPACE DOWN BELOW THAT WILL PUT A HUGE SMILE ON YOUR FACE. ALWAYS TRY TO GO TO BED SMILING AND FEELING HAPPY!

-THINK OF WAYS YOU CAN MAKE YOUR DAY EVEN BETTER TOMORROW.

-ALWAYS SHARE YOUR THOUGHTS AND CONCERNS (even when it is hard to do sometimes) WITH YOUR LOVING FAMILY FOR PROPER GUIDANCE AND GREAT IDEAS. WRITE THEM DOWN BELOW IF NEEDED.

"Sometimes the most important thing you will ever need to learn is how to become your own best friend."(2)

~Anonymous

Date ___/___/20___

STRESSFUL MOMENTS:

_____

_____

_____

HAPPY MOMENTS:

_____

_____

_____

PLAN AHEAD TODAY TO MINIMIZE YOUR STRESS TOMORROW.
(OR YOU CAN JUST WRITE OR DRAW SOMETHING SILLY DOWN BELOW AND GO TO BED SMILING.)
PLANS FOR TOMORROW/TO DO LIST:

CREATE YOUR **OWN** INSPIRING **QUOTE** AND **SHARE YOUR WISDOM** WITH OTHERS!

_____

_____

Date ___/___/20__

STRESSFUL MOMENTS:

_____

_____

HAPPY MOMENTS:

_____

_____

_____

Family Bonding Time...

-WRITE OR DRAW SOMETHING SILLY IN THE SPACE DOWN BELOW THAT WILL PUT A HUGE SMILE ON YOUR FACE. ALWAYS TRY TO GO TO BED SMILING AND FEELING HAPPY!

-THINK OF WAYS YOU CAN MAKE YOUR DAY EVEN BETTER TOMORROW.

-ALWAYS SHARE YOUR THOUGHTS AND CONCERNS (even when it is hard to do sometimes) WITH YOUR LOVING FAMILY FOR PROPER GUIDANCE AND GREAT IDEAS.

WRITE THEM DOWN BELOW IF NEEDED.

"Train your mind to see the good in every situation."(2)   ~unknown

Date ___/___/20__

STRESSFUL MOMENTS:

_____

_____

_____

HAPPY MOMENTS:

_____

_____

_____

PLAN AHEAD TODAY TO MINIMIZE YOUR STRESS TOMORROW.
(OR YOU CAN JUST WRITE OR DRAW SOMETHING SILLY DOWN BELOW AND GO TO
BED SMILING.)
PLANS FOR TOMORROW/TO DO LIST:

Live Your Dreams

Negative people attract negativity. Positive people attract positivity. Surround yourself with positive ones, and try to lose the others.

Date ___/___/20__

STRESSFUL MOMENTS:

_____

_____

_____

HAPPY MOMENTS:

_____

_____

_____

PLAN AHEAD TODAY TO MINIMIZE YOUR STRESS TOMORROW.
(OR YOU CAN JUST WRITE OR DRAW SOMETHING SILLY DOWN BELOW AND GO TO BED SMILING.)
PLANS FOR TOMORROW/TO DO LIST:

CREATE YOUR OWN INSPIRING QUOTE AND SHARE YOUR WISDOM WITH OTHERS!

_____

_____

Date ___/___/20__

STRESSFUL MOMENTS:

_____

_____

HAPPY MOMENTS:

_____

_____

_____

Family Bonding Time...

-WRITE OR DRAW SOMETHING SILLY IN THE SPACE DOWN BELOW THAT WILL PUT A HUGE SMILE ON YOUR FACE. ALWAYS TRY TO GO TO BED SMILING AND FEELING HAPPY!

-THINK OF WAYS YOU CAN MAKE YOUR DAY EVEN BETTER TOMORROW.

-ALWAYS SHARE YOUR THOUGHTS AND CONCERNS (even when it is hard to do sometimes) WITH YOUR LOVING FAMILY FOR PROPER GUIDANCE AND GREAT IDEAS. WRITE THEM DOWN BELOW IF NEEDED.

Never stop chasing your dreams because sometimes what you need is just one more step. Work hard. Failure is not an option - it is a stepping stone to your success.

Date ___ / ___ /20 ___

STRESSFUL MOMENTS:

_____

_____

_____

HAPPY MOMENTS:

_____

_____

_____

PLAN AHEAD TODAY TO MINIMIZE YOUR STRESS TOMORROW.
(OR YOU CAN JUST WRITE OR DRAW SOMETHING SILLY DOWN BELOW AND GO TO BED SMILING.)
PLANS FOR TOMORROW/TO DO LIST:

CREATE YOUR **OWN** INSPIRING **QUOTE** AND **SHARE YOUR WISDOM** WITH OTHERS!

_____

_____

Date ___/___/20__

STRESSFUL MOMENTS:

_____

_____

HAPPY MOMENTS:

_____

_____

Family Bonding Time...

-WRITE OR DRAW SOMETHING SILLY IN THE SPACE DOWN BELOW THAT WILL PUT A HUGE SMILE ON YOUR FACE. ALWAYS TRY TO GO TO BED SMILING AND FEELING HAPPY!

-THINK OF WAYS YOU CAN MAKE YOUR DAY EVEN BETTER TOMORROW.

-ALWAYS SHARE YOUR THOUGHTS AND CONCERNS (even when it is hard to do sometimes) WITH YOUR LOVING FAMILY FOR PROPER GUIDANCE AND GREAT IDEAS. WRITE THEM DOWN BELOW IF NEEDED.

**"The first step is the hardest. The journey of a thousand miles begins with...
One step."**(2)

~unknown

Date ___/___/20___

STRESSFUL MOMENTS:

_____

_____

_____

HAPPY MOMENTS:

_____

_____

_____

PLAN AHEAD TODAY TO MINIMIZE YOUR STRESS TOMORROW.
(OR YOU CAN JUST WRITE OR DRAW SOMETHING SILLY DOWN BELOW AND GO TO
BED SMILING.)
PLANS FOR TOMORROW/TO DO LIST:

CREATE YOUR **OWN** INSPIRING **QUOTE** AND **SHARE YOUR WISDOM WITH OTHERS!**

_____

_____

Date ___/___/20__

STRESSFUL MOMENTS:

_____

_____

HAPPY MOMENTS:

_____

_____

_____

Family Bonding Time...

-WRITE OR DRAW SOMETHING SILLY IN THE SPACE DOWN BELOW THAT WILL PUT A HUGE SMILE ON YOUR FACE. ALWAYS TRY TO GO TO BED SMILING AND FEELING HAPPY!
-THINK OF WAYS YOU CAN MAKE YOUR DAY EVEN BETTER TOMORROW.
-ALWAYS SHARE YOUR THOUGHTS AND CONCERNS (even when it is hard to do sometimes) WITH YOUR LOVING FAMILY FOR PROPER GUIDANCE AND GREAT IDEAS. WRITE THEM DOWN BELOW IF NEEDED.

"Kind words can be short and easy to speak, but their echoes are truly endless."(4)

~Mother Teresa

Date ___/___/20__

STRESSFUL MOMENTS:

_____

_____

_____

HAPPY MOMENTS:

_____

_____

_____

PLAN AHEAD TODAY TO MINIMIZE YOUR STRESS TOMORROW.
(OR YOU CAN JUST WRITE OR DRAW SOMETHING SILLY DOWN BELOW AND GO TO BED SMILING.)
PLANS FOR TOMORROW/TO DO LIST:

CREATE YOUR **OWN** INSPIRING **QUOTE** AND **SHARE YOUR WISDOM** WITH OTHERS!

_____

_____

Date ___ / ___ /20 __

STRESSFUL MOMENTS:

_____

_____

HAPPY MOMENTS:

_____

_____

_____

Family Bonding Time...

-WRITE OR DRAW SOMETHING SILLY IN THE SPACE DOWN BELOW THAT WILL PUT A HUGE SMILE ON YOUR FACE. ALWAYS TRY TO GO TO BED SMILING AND FEELING HAPPY!

-THINK OF WAYS YOU CAN MAKE YOUR DAY EVEN BETTER TOMORROW.

-ALWAYS SHARE YOUR THOUGHTS AND CONCERNS (even when it is hard to do sometimes) WITH YOUR LOVING FAMILY FOR PROPER GUIDANCE AND GREAT IDEAS.

WRITE THEM DOWN BELOW IF NEEDED.

"There are always ten better things to do than just to give up."(2)   ~unknown

Date ___/___/20__

STRESSFUL MOMENTS:

_____

_____

_____

HAPPY MOMENTS:

_____

_____

_____

PLAN AHEAD TODAY TO MINIMIZE YOUR STRESS TOMORROW.
(OR YOU CAN JUST WRITE OR DRAW SOMETHING SILLY DOWN BELOW AND GO TO BED SMILING.)
PLANS FOR TOMORROW/TO DO LIST:

CREATE YOUR **OWN** INSPIRING **QUOTE** AND **SHARE YOUR WISDOM** WITH OTHERS!

_____

_____

Date ___ / ___ /20 ___

STRESSFUL MOMENTS:

_____

_____

HAPPY MOMENTS:

_____

_____

_____

Family Bonding Time...

-**WRITE OR DRAW SOMETHING SILLY IN THE SPACE DOWN BELOW THAT** WILL PUT A HUGE SMILE ON YOUR FACE. ALWAYS TRY TO GO TO BED SMILING AND FEELING HAPPY!
-**THINK** OF WAYS YOU CAN MAKE YOUR DAY EVEN BETTER TOMORROW.
-**ALWAYS SHARE** YOUR THOUGHTS AND CONCERNS (even when it is hard to do sometimes) WITH YOUR LOVING FAMILY FOR PROPER GUIDANCE AND GREAT IDEAS. WRITE THEM DOWN BELOW IF NEEDED.

"Holding on to anger is like grasping a hot coal with the intent of throwing it at someone else; you are the one who gets burned."(2)   ~Buddha

Date ___/___/20___

STRESSFUL MOMENTS:

_____

_____

_____

HAPPY MOMENTS:

_____

_____

_____

PLAN AHEAD TODAY TO MINIMIZE YOUR STRESS TOMORROW.
(OR YOU CAN JUST WRITE OR DRAW SOMETHING SILLY DOWN BELOW AND GO TO BED SMILING.)
PLANS FOR TOMORROW/TO DO LIST:

CREATE YOUR **OWN** INSPIRING **QUOTE** AND **SHARE YOUR WISDOM** WITH OTHERS!

_____

_____

Date ___/___/20__

STRESSFUL MOMENTS:

_____

_____

HAPPY MOMENTS:

_____

_____

Family Bonding Time...

-WRITE OR DRAW SOMETHING SILLY IN THE SPACE DOWN BELOW THAT WILL PUT A HUGE SMILE ON YOUR FACE. ALWAYS TRY TO GO TO BED SMILING AND FEELING HAPPY!

-THINK OF WAYS YOU CAN MAKE YOUR DAY EVEN BETTER TOMORROW.

-ALWAYS SHARE YOUR THOUGHTS AND CONCERNS (even when it is hard to do sometimes) WITH YOUR LOVING FAMILY FOR PROPER GUIDANCE AND GREAT IDEAS.

WRITE THEM DOWN BELOW IF NEEDED.

When you change your mind about stress - you can change your body's response to stress.

Date ___ / ___ /20 __

STRESSFUL MOMENTS:

_____

_____

_____

HAPPY MOMENTS:

_____

_____

_____

PLAN AHEAD TODAY TO MINIMIZE YOUR STRESS TOMORROW.
(OR YOU CAN JUST WRITE OR DRAW SOMETHING SILLY DOWN BELOW AND GO TO BED SMILING.)
PLANS FOR TOMORROW/TO DO LIST:

CREATE YOUR OWN INSPIRING QUOTE AND SHARE YOUR WISDOM WITH OTHERS!

_____

_____

Date ___/___/20___

STRESSFUL MOMENTS:

_____

_____

HAPPY MOMENTS:

_____

_____

_____

Family Bonding Time...

-WRITE OR DRAW SOMETHING SILLY IN THE SPACE DOWN BELOW THAT WILL PUT A HUGE SMILE ON YOUR FACE. ALWAYS TRY TO GO TO BED SMILING AND FEELING HAPPY!

-THINK OF WAYS YOU CAN MAKE YOUR DAY EVEN BETTER TOMORROW.

-ALWAYS SHARE YOUR THOUGHTS AND CONCERNS (even when it is hard to do sometimes) WITH YOUR LOVING FAMILY FOR PROPER GUIDANCE AND GREAT IDEAS.

WRITE THEM DOWN BELOW IF NEEDED.

"Everything happens for a reason... Sometimes good things fall apart so better thing can come together."(2)

                                                                    ~Marilyn Monroe

Date ___/___/20__

STRESSFUL MOMENTS:

_____

_____

_____

HAPPY MOMENTS:

_____

_____

_____

PLAN AHEAD TODAY TO MINIMIZE YOUR STRESS TOMORROW.
(OR YOU CAN JUST WRITE OR DRAW SOMETHING SILLY DOWN BELOW AND GO TO BED SMILING.)
PLANS FOR TOMORROW/TO DO LIST:

                                                                           79

You are Beautiful

You should never let your mind wander into the negative-thoughts zone. Commit to stay focused on happiness and live in the present moment. Yesterday is gone. Tomorrow is not guaranteed. Enjoy your life today!

Date ___/___/20__

STRESSFUL MOMENTS:

_____

_____

_____

HAPPY MOMENTS:

_____

_____

_____

PLAN AHEAD TODAY TO MINIMIZE YOUR STRESS TOMORROW.
(OR YOU CAN JUST WRITE OR DRAW SOMETHING SILLY DOWN BELOW AND GO TO BED SMILING.)
PLANS FOR TOMORROW/TO DO LIST:

CREATE YOUR OWN INSPIRING QUOTE AND SHARE YOUR WISDOM WITH OTHERS!

_____

_____

Date ___/___/20___

STRESSFUL MOMENTS:

_____

_____

HAPPY MOMENTS:

_____

_____

Family Bonding Time...

-WRITE OR DRAW SOMETHING SILLY IN THE SPACE DOWN BELOW THAT WILL PUT A HUGE SMILE ON YOUR FACE. ALWAYS TRY TO GO TO BED SMILING AND FEELING HAPPY!

-THINK OF WAYS YOU CAN MAKE YOUR DAY EVEN BETTER TOMORROW.

-ALWAYS SHARE YOUR THOUGHTS AND CONCERNS (even when it is hard to do sometimes) WITH YOUR LOVING FAMILY FOR PROPER GUIDANCE AND GREAT IDEAS.

WRITE THEM DOWN BELOW IF NEEDED.

Do at least ONE thing just for YOU daily!

Date ___/___/20__

STRESSFUL MOMENTS:

_____

_____

_____

HAPPY MOMENTS:

_____

_____

_____

PLAN AHEAD TODAY TO MINIMIZE YOUR STRESS TOMORROW.
(OR YOU CAN JUST WRITE OR DRAW SOMETHING SILLY DOWN BELOW AND GO TO
BED SMILING.)
PLANS FOR TOMORROW/TO DO LIST:

CREATE YOUR OWN INSPIRING QUOTE AND SHARE YOUR WISDOM WITH OTHERS!

_____

_____

Date ___/___/20__

STRESSFUL MOMENTS:

_____

_____

HAPPY MOMENTS:

_____

_____

_____

Family Bonding Time…

-WRITE OR DRAW SOMETHING SILLY IN THE SPACE DOWN BELOW THAT WILL PUT A HUGE SMILE ON YOUR FACE. ALWAYS TRY TO GO TO BED SMILING AND FEELING HAPPY!

-THINK OF WAYS YOU CAN MAKE YOUR DAY EVEN BETTER TOMORROW.

-ALWAYS SHARE YOUR THOUGHTS AND CONCERNS (even when it is hard to do sometimes) WITH YOUR LOVING FAMILY FOR PROPER GUIDANCE AND GREAT IDEAS. WRITE THEM DOWN BELOW IF NEEDED.

"Education is the ability to listen to almost anything without losing your temper or your self-confidence."(1)

~Robert Frost

Date ___ / ___ /20 __

STRESSFUL MOMENTS:

_____

_____

_____

HAPPY MOMENTS:

_____

_____

_____

PLAN AHEAD TODAY TO MINIMIZE YOUR STRESS TOMORROW.
(OR YOU CAN JUST WRITE OR DRAW SOMETHING SILLY DOWN BELOW AND GO TO BED SMILING.)
PLANS FOR TOMORROW/TO DO LIST:

CREATE YOUR OWN INSPIRING QUOTE AND SHARE YOUR WISDOM WITH OTHERS!

_____

_____

Date ___/___/20__

STRESSFUL MOMENTS:

_____

_____

HAPPY MOMENTS:

_____

_____

Family Bonding Time...

-WRITE OR DRAW SOMETHING SILLY IN THE SPACE DOWN BELOW THAT WILL PUT A HUGE SMILE ON YOUR FACE. ALWAYS TRY TO GO TO BED SMILING AND FEELING HAPPY!

-THINK OF WAYS YOU CAN MAKE YOUR DAY EVEN BETTER TOMORROW.

-ALWAYS SHARE YOUR THOUGHTS AND CONCERNS (even when it is hard to do sometimes) WITH YOUR LOVING FAMILY FOR PROPER GUIDANCE AND GREAT IDEAS. WRITE THEM DOWN BELOW IF NEEDED.

"Laugh when you can, apologize when you should, and let go of what you can't change. Life's too short to be anything... but happy."(2)

- Anonymous

Date ___/___/20__

STRESSFUL MOMENTS:

_____

_____

_____

HAPPY MOMENTS:

_____

_____

_____

PLAN AHEAD TODAY TO MINIMIZE YOUR STRESS TOMORROW.
(OR YOU CAN JUST WRITE OR DRAW SOMETHING SILLY DOWN BELOW AND GO TO BED SMILING.)
PLANS FOR TOMORROW/TO DO LIST:

CREATE YOUR OWN INSPIRING QUOTE AND SHARE YOUR WISDOM WITH OTHERS!

_____

_____

Date ___/___/20__

STRESSFUL MOMENTS:

_____

_____

HAPPY MOMENTS:

_____

_____

_____

Family Bonding Time…

-WRITE OR DRAW SOMETHING SILLY IN THE SPACE DOWN BELOW THAT WILL PUT A HUGE SMILE ON YOUR FACE. ALWAYS TRY TO GO TO BED SMILING AND FEELING HAPPY!

-THINK OF WAYS YOU CAN MAKE YOUR DAY EVEN BETTER TOMORROW.

-ALWAYS SHARE YOUR THOUGHTS AND CONCERNS (even when it is hard to do sometimes) WITH YOUR LOVING FAMILY FOR PROPER GUIDANCE AND GREAT IDEAS. WRITE THEM DOWN BELOW IF NEEDED.

Enjoy your life today! Live in the present moment.

Date ___/___/20__

STRESSFUL MOMENTS:

_____

_____

_____

HAPPY MOMENTS:

_____

_____

_____

PLAN AHEAD TODAY TO MINIMIZE YOUR STRESS TOMORROW.
(OR YOU CAN JUST WRITE OR DRAW SOMETHING SILLY DOWN BELOW AND GO TO BED SMILING.)
PLANS FOR TOMORROW/TO DO LIST:

CREATE YOUR OWN INSPIRING QUOTE AND SHARE YOUR WISDOM WITH OTHERS!

_____

_____

Date ___/___/20__

STRESSFUL MOMENTS:

_____

_____

HAPPY MOMENTS:

_____

_____

Family Bonding Time…

-WRITE OR DRAW SOMETHING SILLY IN THE SPACE DOWN BELOW THAT WILL PUT A HUGE SMILE ON YOUR FACE. ALWAYS TRY TO GO TO BED SMILING AND FEELING HAPPY!

-THINK OF WAYS YOU CAN MAKE YOUR DAY EVEN BETTER TOMORROW.

-ALWAYS SHARE YOUR THOUGHTS AND CONCERNS (even when it is hard to do sometimes) WITH YOUR LOVING FAMILY FOR PROPER GUIDANCE AND GREAT IDEAS.

WRITE THEM DOWN BELOW IF NEEDED.

"You grow up the day you have your first real laugh – at yourself."[1]

~Ethel Barrymore

Date ___/___/20__

STRESSFUL MOMENTS:

_____

_____

_____

HAPPY MOMENTS:

_____

_____

_____

PLAN AHEAD TODAY TO MINIMIZE YOUR STRESS TOMORROW.
(OR YOU CAN JUST WRITE OR DRAW SOMETHING SILLY DOWN BELOW AND GO TO
BED SMILING.)
PLANS FOR TOMORROW/TO DO LIST:

CREATE YOUR OWN INSPIRING QUOTE AND SHARE YOUR WISDOM WITH OTHERS!

_____

_____

Date ___/___/20__

STRESSFUL MOMENTS:

_____

_____

HAPPY MOMENTS:

_____

_____

Family Bonding Time...

-WRITE OR DRAW SOMETHING SILLY IN THE SPACE DOWN BELOW THAT WILL PUT A HUGE SMILE ON YOUR FACE. ALWAYS TRY TO GO TO BED SMILING AND FEELING HAPPY!

-THINK OF WAYS YOU CAN MAKE YOUR DAY EVEN BETTER TOMORROW.

-ALWAYS SHARE YOUR THOUGHTS AND CONCERNS (even when it is hard to do sometimes) WITH YOUR LOVING FAMILY FOR PROPER GUIDANCE AND GREAT IDEAS. WRITE THEM DOWN BELOW IF NEEDED.

"Take a deep breath. It's just a bad day, not a bad life."(2)   ~unknown

Date ___/___/20__

STRESSFUL MOMENTS:

_____

_____

_____

HAPPY MOMENTS:

_____

_____

_____

PLAN AHEAD TODAY TO MINIMIZE YOUR STRESS TOMORROW.
(OR YOU CAN JUST WRITE OR DRAW SOMETHING SILLY DOWN BELOW AND GO TO BED SMILING.)
PLANS FOR TOMORROW/TO DO LIST:

Do what makes you Happy

"A friend to all is a friend to none."(1)   ~Aristotle

Date ___/___/20__

STRESSFUL MOMENTS:

_____

_____

_____

HAPPY MOMENTS:

_____

_____

_____

PLAN AHEAD TODAY TO MINIMIZE YOUR STRESS TOMORROW.
(OR YOU CAN JUST WRITE OR DRAW SOMETHING SILLY DOWN BELOW AND GO TO
BED SMILING.)
PLANS FOR TOMORROW/TO DO LIST:

CREATE YOUR OWN INSPIRING QUOTE AND SHARE YOUR WISDOM WITH OTHERS!

_____

_____

Date ___/___/20__

STRESSFUL MOMENTS:

_____

_____

HAPPY MOMENTS:

_____

_____

Family Bonding Time...

-WRITE OR DRAW SOMETHING SILLY IN THE SPACE DOWN BELOW THAT WILL PUT A HUGE SMILE ON YOUR FACE. ALWAYS TRY TO GO TO BED SMILING AND FEELING HAPPY!

-THINK OF WAYS YOU CAN MAKE YOUR DAY EVEN BETTER TOMORROW.

-ALWAYS SHARE YOUR THOUGHTS AND CONCERNS (even when it is hard to do sometimes) WITH YOUR LOVING FAMILY FOR PROPER GUIDANCE AND GREAT IDEAS. WRITE THEM DOWN BELOW IF NEEDED.

"Anger is an acid that can do more harm to the vessel in which it is stored than to anything on which it is poured."(2)

~Mark Twain

Date ___/___/20__

STRESSFUL MOMENTS:

_____

_____

_____

HAPPY MOMENTS:

_____

_____

_____

PLAN AHEAD TODAY TO MINIMIZE YOUR STRESS TOMORROW.
(OR YOU CAN JUST WRITE OR DRAW SOMETHING SILLY DOWN BELOW AND GO TO BED SMILING.)
PLANS FOR TOMORROW/TO DO LIST:

CREATE YOUR OWN INSPIRING QUOTE AND SHARE YOUR WISDOM WITH OTHERS!

_____

_____

Date ___ / ___ /20___

STRESSFUL MOMENTS:

_____

_____

HAPPY MOMENTS:

_____

_____

_____

Family Bonding Time...

-WRITE OR DRAW SOMETHING SILLY IN THE SPACE DOWN BELOW THAT WILL PUT A HUGE SMILE ON YOUR FACE. ALWAYS TRY TO GO TO BED SMILING AND FEELING HAPPY!

-THINK OF WAYS YOU CAN MAKE YOUR DAY EVEN BETTER TOMORROW.

-ALWAYS SHARE YOUR THOUGHTS AND CONCERNS (even when it is hard to do sometimes) WITH YOUR LOVING FAMILY FOR PROPER GUIDANCE AND GREAT IDEAS.

WRITE THEM DOWN BELOW IF NEEDED.

"Be with those who bring out the best in you, not the stress in you."(2)
~unknown

Date ___/___/20__

STRESSFUL MOMENTS:

_____

_____

_____

HAPPY MOMENTS:

_____

_____

_____

PLAN AHEAD TODAY TO MINIMIZE YOUR STRESS TOMORROW.
(OR YOU CAN JUST WRITE OR DRAW SOMETHING SILLY DOWN BELOW AND GO TO
BED SMILING.)
PLANS FOR TOMORROW/TO DO LIST:

CREATE YOUR OWN INSPIRING QUOTE AND SHARE YOUR WISDOM WITH OTHERS!

_____

_____

Date ___ / ___ /20___

STRESSFUL MOMENTS:

_____

_____

HAPPY MOMENTS:

_____

_____

_____

Family Bonding Time...

-WRITE OR DRAW SOMETHING SILLY IN THE SPACE DOWN BELOW THAT WILL PUT A HUGE SMILE ON YOUR FACE. ALWAYS TRY TO GO TO BED SMILING AND FEELING HAPPY!

-THINK OF WAYS YOU CAN MAKE YOUR DAY EVEN BETTER TOMORROW.

-ALWAYS SHARE YOUR THOUGHTS AND CONCERNS (even when it is hard to do sometimes) WITH YOUR LOVING FAMILY FOR PROPER GUIDANCE AND GREAT IDEAS. WRITE THEM DOWN BELOW IF NEEDED.

"Develop success from failures. Discouragement and failure are two of the surest stepping stones to success."(1)

~Dale Carnegie

Date ___/___/20__

STRESSFUL MOMENTS:

_____

_____

_____

HAPPY MOMENTS:

_____

_____

_____

PLAN AHEAD TODAY TO MINIMIZE YOUR STRESS TOMORROW.

(OR YOU CAN JUST WRITE OR DRAW SOMETHING SILLY DOWN BELOW AND GO TO BED SMILING.)

PLANS FOR TOMORROW/TO DO LIST:

CREATE YOUR OWN INSPIRING QUOTE AND SHARE YOUR WISDOM WITH OTHERS!

_____

_____

Date ___/___/20__

STRESSFUL MOMENTS:

_____

_____

HAPPY MOMENTS:

_____

_____

Family Bonding Time...

-WRITE OR DRAW SOMETHING SILLY IN THE SPACE DOWN BELOW THAT WILL PUT A HUGE SMILE ON YOUR FACE. ALWAYS TRY TO GO TO BED SMILING AND FEELING HAPPY!

-THINK OF WAYS YOU CAN MAKE YOUR DAY EVEN BETTER TOMORROW.

-ALWAYS SHARE YOUR THOUGHTS AND CONCERNS (even when it is hard to do sometimes) WITH YOUR LOVING FAMILY FOR PROPER GUIDANCE AND GREAT IDEAS. WRITE THEM DOWN BELOW IF NEEDED.

IMAGINE... BELIEVE... ACHIEVE!

Date ___/___/20__

STRESSFUL MOMENTS:

_____

_____

_____

HAPPY MOMENTS:

_____

_____

_____

PLAN AHEAD TODAY TO MINIMIZE YOUR STRESS TOMORROW.
(OR YOU CAN JUST WRITE OR DRAW SOMETHING SILLY DOWN BELOW AND GO TO BED SMILING.)
PLANS FOR TOMORROW/TO DO LIST:

CREATE YOUR OWN INSPIRING QUOTE AND SHARE YOUR WISDOM WITH OTHERS!

_____

_____

Date ___/___/20__

STRESSFUL MOMENTS:

_____

_____

HAPPY MOMENTS:

_____

_____

Family Bonding Time...

-WRITE OR DRAW SOMETHING SILLY IN THE SPACE DOWN BELOW THAT WILL PUT A HUGE SMILE ON YOUR FACE. ALWAYS TRY TO GO TO BED SMILING AND FEELING HAPPY!

-THINK OF WAYS YOU CAN MAKE YOUR DAY EVEN BETTER TOMORROW.

-ALWAYS SHARE YOUR THOUGHTS AND CONCERNS (even when it is hard to do sometimes) WITH YOUR LOVING FAMILY FOR PROPER GUIDANCE AND GREAT IDEAS. WRITE THEM DOWN BELOW IF NEEDED.

Waking up in the morning and thinking about what you are grateful for is so important. Start listing in your head what you are thankful for TODAY. This is a great habit that will fill you with positive energy for the rest of the day!

Date ___/___/20__

STRESSFUL MOMENTS:

_____

_____

_____

HAPPY MOMENTS:

_____

_____

_____

PLAN AHEAD TODAY TO MINIMIZE YOUR STRESS TOMORROW.
(OR YOU CAN JUST WRITE OR DRAW SOMETHING SILLY DOWN BELOW AND GO TO BED SMILING.)
PLANS FOR TOMORROW/TO DO LIST:

CREATE YOUR OWN INSPIRING QUOTE AND SHARE YOUR WISDOM WITH OTHERS!

_____

_____

Date ___/___/20__

STRESSFUL MOMENTS:

_____

_____

HAPPY MOMENTS:

_____

_____

_____

Family Bonding Time...

-WRITE OR DRAW SOMETHING SILLY IN THE SPACE DOWN BELOW THAT WILL PUT A HUGE SMILE ON YOUR FACE. ALWAYS TRY TO GO TO BED SMILING AND FEELING HAPPY!

-THINK OF WAYS YOU CAN MAKE YOUR DAY EVEN BETTER TOMORROW.

-ALWAYS SHARE YOUR THOUGHTS AND CONCERNS (even when it is hard to do sometimes) WITH YOUR LOVING FAMILY FOR PROPER GUIDANCE AND GREAT IDEAS. WRITE THEM DOWN BELOW IF NEEDED.

"I am not what happened to me, I am what I choose to be."(1)   ~Carl Jung

Date ___/___/20__

STRESSFUL MOMENTS:

_____

_____

_____

HAPPY MOMENTS:

_____

_____

_____

PLAN AHEAD TODAY TO MINIMIZE YOUR STRESS TOMORROW.
(OR YOU CAN JUST WRITE OR DRAW SOMETHING SILLY DOWN BELOW AND GO TO
BED SMILING.)
PLANS FOR TOMORROW/TO DO LIST:

CREATE YOUR OWN INSPIRING QUOTE AND SHARE YOUR WISDOM WITH OTHERS!

_____

_____

Date ___/___/20__

STRESSFUL MOMENTS:

_____

_____

HAPPY MOMENTS:

_____

_____

Family Bonding Time...

-WRITE OR DRAW SOMETHING SILLY IN THE SPACE DOWN BELOW THAT WILL PUT A HUGE SMILE ON YOUR FACE. ALWAYS TRY TO GO TO BED SMILING AND FEELING HAPPY!

-THINK OF WAYS YOU CAN MAKE YOUR DAY EVEN BETTER TOMORROW.

-ALWAYS SHARE YOUR THOUGHTS AND CONCERNS (even when it is hard to do sometimes) WITH YOUR LOVING FAMILY FOR PROPER GUIDANCE AND GREAT IDEAS.

WRITE THEM DOWN BELOW IF NEEDED.

Don't let your mind be your own limitation. Learn about the power of your mind and stay in control. Limit negativity around you. Focus on your happiness and positive attitude.

Date ___ / ___ /20__

STRESSFUL MOMENTS:

_____

_____

_____

HAPPY MOMENTS:

_____

_____

_____

PLAN AHEAD TODAY TO MINIMIZE YOUR STRESS TOMORROW.
(OR YOU CAN JUST WRITE OR DRAW SOMETHING SILLY DOWN BELOW AND GO TO BED SMILING.)
PLANS FOR TOMORROW/TO DO LIST:

Success
is the only
option

"Being strong doesn't always mean you have to fight the battle. True strength is being adult enough to walk away from the nonsense with your head held high."(2)   ~unknown

Date ___/___/20__

STRESSFUL MOMENTS:

_____

_____

_____

HAPPY MOMENTS:

_____

_____

_____

PLAN AHEAD TODAY TO MINIMIZE YOUR STRESS TOMORROW.
(OR YOU CAN JUST WRITE OR DRAW SOMETHING SILLY DOWN BELOW AND GO TO BED SMILING.)
PLANS FOR TOMORROW/TO DO LIST:

CREATE YOUR OWN INSPIRING QUOTE AND SHARE YOUR WISDOM WITH OTHERS!

_____

_____

Date ___/___/20__

STRESSFUL MOMENTS:

_____

_____

HAPPY MOMENTS:

_____

_____

Family Bonding Time...

-WRITE OR DRAW SOMETHING SILLY IN THE SPACE DOWN BELOW THAT WILL PUT A HUGE SMILE ON YOUR FACE. ALWAYS TRY TO GO TO BED SMILING AND FEELING HAPPY!

-THINK OF WAYS YOU CAN MAKE YOUR DAY EVEN BETTER TOMORROW.

-ALWAYS SHARE YOUR THOUGHTS AND CONCERNS (even when it is hard to do sometimes) WITH YOUR LOVING FAMILY FOR PROPER GUIDANCE AND GREAT IDEAS. WRITE THEM DOWN BELOW IF NEEDED.

"When you start to wonder whether you can trust someone or not, that is when you already know you don't."(2)

~unknown

Date ___/___/20__

STRESSFUL MOMENTS:

_____

_____

_____

HAPPY MOMENTS:

_____

_____

_____

PLAN AHEAD TODAY TO MINIMIZE YOUR STRESS TOMORROW.

(OR YOU CAN JUST WRITE OR DRAW SOMETHING SILLY DOWN BELOW AND GO TO BED SMILING.)

PLANS FOR TOMORROW/TO DO LIST:

CREATE YOUR **OWN** INSPIRING **QUOTE** AND **SHARE YOUR WISDOM** WITH OTHERS!

_____

_____

Date ___/___/20__

STRESSFUL MOMENTS:

_____

_____

HAPPY MOMENTS:

_____

_____

Family Bonding Time...

-WRITE OR DRAW SOMETHING SILLY IN THE SPACE DOWN BELOW THAT WILL PUT A HUGE SMILE ON YOUR FACE. ALWAYS TRY TO GO TO BED SMILING AND FEELING HAPPY!

-THINK OF WAYS YOU CAN MAKE YOUR DAY EVEN BETTER TOMORROW.

-ALWAYS SHARE YOUR THOUGHTS AND CONCERNS (even when it is hard to do sometimes) WITH YOUR LOVING FAMILY FOR PROPER GUIDANCE AND GREAT IDEAS. WRITE THEM DOWN BELOW IF NEEDED.

"Worrying doesn't take away tomorrow's trouble. It takes away today's peace."(2)

~Anonymous

Date ___/___/20__

STRESSFUL MOMENTS:

_____

_____

_____

HAPPY MOMENTS:

_____

_____

_____

PLAN AHEAD TODAY TO MINIMIZE YOUR STRESS TOMORROW.
(OR YOU CAN JUST WRITE OR DRAW SOMETHING SILLY DOWN BELOW AND GO TO BED SMILING.)
PLANS FOR TOMORROW/TO DO LIST:

CREATE YOUR **OWN** INSPIRING **QUOTE** AND **SHARE YOUR WISDOM** WITH OTHERS!

_____

_____

Date ___/___/20__

STRESSFUL MOMENTS:

_____

_____

HAPPY MOMENTS:

_____

_____

_____

Family Bonding Time...

-WRITE OR DRAW SOMETHING SILLY IN THE SPACE DOWN BELOW THAT WILL PUT A HUGE SMILE ON YOUR FACE. ALWAYS TRY TO GO TO BED SMILING AND FEELING HAPPY!

-THINK OF WAYS YOU CAN MAKE YOUR DAY EVEN BETTER TOMORROW.

-ALWAYS SHARE YOUR THOUGHTS AND CONCERNS (even when it is hard to do sometimes) WITH YOUR LOVING FAMILY FOR PROPER GUIDANCE AND GREAT IDEAS. WRITE THEM DOWN BELOW IF NEEDED.

"The secret of getting ahead is getting started. The secret of getting started is breaking your complex overwhelming tasks into manageable tasks, and then starting on the first one."[1]   ~Mark Twain

Date ___/___/20___

STRESSFUL MOMENTS:

_____

_____

_____

HAPPY MOMENTS:

_____

_____

_____

PLAN AHEAD TODAY TO MINIMIZE YOUR STRESS TOMORROW.
(OR YOU CAN JUST WRITE OR DRAW SOMETHING SILLY DOWN BELOW AND GO TO BED SMILING.)
PLANS FOR TOMORROW/TO DO LIST:

CREATE YOUR OWN INSPIRING QUOTE AND SHARE YOUR WISDOM WITH OTHERS!

_____

_____

Date ___/___/20__

STRESSFUL MOMENTS:

_____

_____

HAPPY MOMENTS:

_____

_____

_____

Family Bonding Time...

-WRITE OR DRAW SOMETHING SILLY IN THE SPACE DOWN BELOW THAT WILL PUT A HUGE SMILE ON YOUR FACE. ALWAYS TRY TO GO TO BED SMILING AND FEELING HAPPY!

-THINK OF WAYS YOU CAN MAKE YOUR DAY EVEN BETTER TOMORROW.

-ALWAYS SHARE YOUR THOUGHTS AND CONCERNS (even when it is hard to do sometimes) WITH YOUR LOVING FAMILY FOR PROPER GUIDANCE AND GREAT IDEAS. WRITE THEM DOWN BELOW IF NEEDED.

"Promise me you'll always remember: You're braver than you believe, and stronger than you seem, and smarter than you think."(2)

~A.A.Milne

Date ___/___/20___

STRESSFUL MOMENTS:

_____

_____

_____

HAPPY MOMENTS:

_____

_____

_____

PLAN AHEAD TODAY TO MINIMIZE YOUR STRESS TOMORROW.
(OR YOU CAN JUST WRITE OR DRAW SOMETHING SILLY DOWN BELOW AND GO TO BED SMILING.)
PLANS FOR TOMORROW/TO DO LIST:

CREATE YOUR **OWN** INSPIRING **QUOTE** AND **SHARE YOUR WISDOM** WITH OTHERS!

_____

_____

Date ___/___/20___

STRESSFUL MOMENTS:

_____

_____

HAPPY MOMENTS:

_____

_____

Family Bonding Time...

-WRITE OR DRAW SOMETHING SILLY IN THE SPACE DOWN BELOW THAT WILL PUT A HUGE SMILE ON YOUR FACE. ALWAYS TRY TO GO TO BED SMILING AND FEELING HAPPY!

-THINK OF WAYS YOU CAN MAKE YOUR DAY EVEN BETTER TOMORROW.

-ALWAYS SHARE YOUR THOUGHTS AND CONCERNS (even when it is hard to do sometimes) WITH YOUR LOVING FAMILY FOR PROPER GUIDANCE AND GREAT IDEAS. WRITE THEM DOWN BELOW IF NEEDED.

Never waste your feelings and your precious time on someone who doesn't value them.

Date ___/___/20__

STRESSFUL MOMENTS:

_____

_____

_____

HAPPY MOMENTS:

_____

_____

_____

PLAN AHEAD TODAY TO MINIMIZE YOUR STRESS TOMORROW.
(OR YOU CAN JUST WRITE OR DRAW SOMETHING SILLY DOWN BELOW AND GO TO BED SMILING.)
PLANS FOR TOMORROW/TO DO LIST:

CREATE YOUR OWN INSPIRING QUOTE AND SHARE YOUR WISDOM WITH OTHERS!

_____

_____

Date ___/___/20__

STRESSFUL MOMENTS:

_____

_____

HAPPY MOMENTS:

_____

_____

_____

Family Bonding Time...

-WRITE OR DRAW SOMETHING SILLY IN THE SPACE DOWN BELOW THAT WILL PUT A HUGE SMILE ON YOUR FACE. ALWAYS TRY TO GO TO BED SMILING AND FEELING HAPPY!

-THINK OF WAYS YOU CAN MAKE YOUR DAY EVEN BETTER TOMORROW.

-ALWAYS SHARE YOUR THOUGHTS AND CONCERNS (even when it is hard to do sometimes) WITH YOUR LOVING FAMILY FOR PROPER GUIDANCE AND GREAT IDEAS.

WRITE THEM DOWN BELOW IF NEEDED.

When something bad happens in your life, don't try to solve the problem right away. Take a deep breath, analyze it, and only then try to think about possible solutions. I am sure you will find the right one!

Date ___/___/20__

STRESSFUL MOMENTS:

_____

_____

_____

HAPPY MOMENTS:

_____

_____

_____

PLAN AHEAD TODAY TO MINIMIZE YOUR STRESS TOMORROW.
(OR YOU CAN JUST WRITE OR DRAW SOMETHING SILLY DOWN BELOW AND GO TO BED SMILING.)
PLANS FOR TOMORROW/TO DO LIST:

CREATE YOUR OWN INSPIRING QUOTE AND SHARE YOUR WISDOM WITH OTHERS!

_____

_____

Date ___/___/20__

STRESSFUL MOMENTS:

_____

_____

HAPPY MOMENTS:

_____

_____

_____

Family Bonding Time...

-WRITE OR DRAW SOMETHING SILLY IN THE SPACE DOWN BELOW THAT WILL PUT A HUGE SMILE ON YOUR FACE. ALWAYS TRY TO GO TO BED SMILING AND FEELING HAPPY!

-THINK OF WAYS YOU CAN MAKE YOUR DAY EVEN BETTER TOMORROW.

-ALWAYS SHARE YOUR THOUGHTS AND CONCERNS (even when it is hard to do sometimes) WITH YOUR LOVING FAMILY FOR PROPER GUIDANCE AND GREAT IDEAS. WRITE THEM DOWN BELOW IF NEEDED.

Stay away from the people who bring negativity into your life. Embrace your positive thoughts. Stay with friends who put a smile on your face!

Date ___/___/20__

STRESSFUL MOMENTS:

_____

_____

_____

HAPPY MOMENTS:

_____

_____

_____

PLAN AHEAD TODAY TO MINIMIZE YOUR STRESS TOMORROW.
(OR YOU CAN JUST WRITE OR DRAW SOMETHING SILLY DOWN BELOW AND GO TO BED SMILING.)
PLANS FOR TOMORROW/TO DO LIST:

CREATE YOUR **OWN** INSPIRING **QUOTE** AND **SHARE YOUR WISDOM**
WITH OTHERS!

_____

_____

Date ___/___/20__

STRESSFUL MOMENTS:

_____

_____

HAPPY MOMENTS:

_____

_____

_____

Family Bonding Time...

-WRITE OR DRAW SOMETHING SILLY IN THE SPACE DOWN BELOW THAT WILL
PUT A HUGE SMILE ON YOUR FACE. ALWAYS TRY TO GO TO BED SMILING AND
FEELING HAPPY!
-THINK OF WAYS YOU CAN MAKE YOUR DAY EVEN BETTER TOMORROW.
-ALWAYS SHARE YOUR THOUGHTS AND CONCERNS (even when it is hard to do
sometimes) WITH YOUR LOVING FAMILY FOR PROPER GUIDANCE AND GREAT IDEAS.
WRITE THEM DOWN BELOW IF NEEDED.

It is so important to practice self love! Stay true to yourself and focus on every positive moment. You will become a "human magnet" to people with the same positive attitude!

Date ___/___/20__

STRESSFUL MOMENTS:

_____

_____

_____

HAPPY MOMENTS:

_____

_____

_____

PLAN AHEAD TODAY TO MINIMIZE YOUR STRESS TOMORROW.
(OR YOU CAN JUST WRITE OR DRAW SOMETHING SILLY DOWN BELOW AND GO TO BED SMILING.)

PLANS FOR TOMORROW/TO DO LIST:

CREATE YOUR OWN INSPIRING QUOTE AND SHARE YOUR WISDOM WITH OTHERS!

_____

_____

Date ___/___/20__

STRESSFUL MOMENTS:

_____

_____

HAPPY MOMENTS:

_____

_____

Family Bonding Time...

-WRITE OR DRAW SOMETHING SILLY IN THE SPACE DOWN BELOW THAT WILL PUT A HUGE SMILE ON YOUR FACE. ALWAYS TRY TO GO TO BED SMILING AND FEELING HAPPY!

-THINK OF WAYS YOU CAN MAKE YOUR DAY EVEN BETTER TOMORROW.

-ALWAYS SHARE YOUR THOUGHTS AND CONCERNS (even when it is hard to do sometimes) WITH YOUR LOVING FAMILY FOR PROPER GUIDANCE AND GREAT IDEAS. WRITE THEM DOWN BELOW IF NEEDED.

Be a leader, not a follower. Teach your friends and family how to be and stay happy!

Date ___/___/20__

STRESSFUL MOMENTS:

_____

_____

_____

HAPPY MOMENTS:

_____

_____

_____

PLAN AHEAD TODAY TO MINIMIZE YOUR STRESS TOMORROW.
(OR YOU CAN JUST WRITE OR DRAW SOMETHING SILLY DOWN BELOW AND GO TO BED SMILING.)
PLANS FOR TOMORROW/TO DO LIST:

CREATE YOUR **OWN** INSPIRING **QUOTE** AND **SHARE YOUR WISDOM** WITH OTHERS!

_____

_____

Date ___/___/20__

STRESSFUL MOMENTS:

_____

_____

HAPPY MOMENTS:

_____

_____

_____

Family Bonding Time...

-WRITE OR DRAW SOMETHING SILLY IN THE SPACE DOWN BELOW THAT WILL PUT A HUGE SMILE ON YOUR FACE. ALWAYS TRY TO GO TO BED SMILING AND FEELING HAPPY!

-THINK OF WAYS YOU CAN MAKE YOUR DAY EVEN BETTER TOMORROW.

-ALWAYS SHARE YOUR THOUGHTS AND CONCERNS (even when it is hard to do sometimes) WITH YOUR LOVING FAMILY FOR PROPER GUIDANCE AND GREAT IDEAS. WRITE THEM DOWN BELOW IF NEEDED.

Share your knowledge of how you've learned to be in control of your own emotions and happiness!

Date ___/___/20__

STRESSFUL MOMENTS:

_____

_____

_____

HAPPY MOMENTS:

_____

_____

_____

PLAN AHEAD TODAY TO MINIMIZE YOUR STRESS TOMORROW.
(OR YOU CAN JUST WRITE OR DRAW SOMETHING SILLY DOWN BELOW AND GO TO BED SMILING.)
PLANS FOR TOMORROW/TO DO LIST:

CREATE YOUR **OWN** INSPIRING **QUOTE** AND **SHARE YOUR WISDOM** WITH OTHERS!

_____

_____

Date ___/___/20__

STRESSFUL MOMENTS:

_____

_____

HAPPY MOMENTS:

_____

_____

_____

Family Bonding Time...

-WRITE OR DRAW SOMETHING SILLY IN THE SPACE DOWN BELOW THAT WILL PUT A HUGE SMILE ON YOUR FACE. ALWAYS TRY TO GO TO BED SMILING AND FEELING HAPPY!

-THINK OF WAYS YOU CAN MAKE YOUR DAY EVEN BETTER TOMORROW.

-ALWAYS SHARE YOUR THOUGHTS AND CONCERNS (even when it is hard to do sometimes) WITH YOUR LOVING FAMILY FOR PROPER GUIDANCE AND GREAT IDEAS. WRITE THEM DOWN BELOW IF NEEDED.

Date ___/___/20__

STRESSFUL MOMENTS:

_____

_____

_____

HAPPY MOMENTS:

_____

_____

_____

PLAN AHEAD TODAY TO MINIMIZE YOUR STRESS TOMORROW.
(OR YOU CAN JUST WRITE OR DRAW SOMETHING SILLY DOWN BELOW AND GO TO
BED SMILING.)
PLANS FOR TOMORROW/TO DO LIST:

CREATE YOUR OWN INSPIRING QUOTE AND SHARE YOUR WISDOM WITH OTHERS!

_____

_____

Date ___/___/20__

STRESSFUL MOMENTS:

_____

_____

HAPPY MOMENTS:

_____

_____

_____

Family Bonding Time...

-WRITE OR DRAW SOMETHING SILLY IN THE SPACE DOWN BELOW THAT WILL PUT A HUGE SMILE ON YOUR FACE. ALWAYS TRY TO GO TO BED SMILING AND FEELING HAPPY!

-THINK OF WAYS YOU CAN MAKE YOUR DAY EVEN BETTER TOMORROW.

-ALWAYS SHARE YOUR THOUGHTS AND CONCERNS (even when it is hard to do sometimes) WITH YOUR LOVING FAMILY FOR PROPER GUIDANCE AND GREAT IDEAS. WRITE THEM DOWN BELOW IF NEEDED.

"Don't let someone dim your light, simply because it's shining in their eyes."(2)

~unknown

Date ___/___/20__

STRESSFUL MOMENTS:

_____

_____

_____

HAPPY MOMENTS:

_____

_____

_____

PLAN AHEAD TODAY TO MINIMIZE YOUR STRESS TOMORROW.
(OR YOU CAN JUST WRITE OR DRAW SOMETHING SILLY DOWN BELOW AND GO TO BED SMILING.)
PLANS FOR TOMORROW/TO DO LIST:

no matter what people tell you, words and ideas can change the world - Robin Williams

"Some people come into your life as Blessings...others as lessons."(2)

~unknown

Date ___ / ___ /20 __

STRESSFUL MOMENTS:

_____

_____

_____

HAPPY MOMENTS:

_____

_____

_____

PLAN AHEAD TODAY TO MINIMIZE YOUR STRESS TOMORROW.
(OR YOU CAN JUST WRITE OR DRAW SOMETHING SILLY DOWN BELOW AND GO TO BED SMILING.)
PLANS FOR TOMORROW/TO DO LIST:

CREATE YOUR OWN INSPIRING QUOTE AND SHARE YOUR WISDOM WITH OTHERS!

_____

_____

Date ___/___/20__

STRESSFUL MOMENTS:

_____

_____

HAPPY MOMENTS:

_____

_____

_____

Family Bonding Time...

-WRITE OR DRAW SOMETHING SILLY IN THE SPACE DOWN BELOW THAT WILL PUT A HUGE SMILE ON YOUR FACE. ALWAYS TRY TO GO TO BED SMILING AND FEELING HAPPY!

-THINK OF WAYS YOU CAN MAKE YOUR DAY EVEN BETTER TOMORROW.

-ALWAYS SHARE YOUR THOUGHTS AND CONCERNS (even when it is hard to do sometimes) WITH YOUR LOVING FAMILY FOR PROPER GUIDANCE AND GREAT IDEAS.

WRITE THEM DOWN BELOW IF NEEDED.

"Every moment is unique... Never before, never again. Enjoy your life today."(2)

~unknown

Date ___/___/20__

STRESSFUL MOMENTS:

_____

_____

_____

HAPPY MOMENTS:

_____

_____

_____

PLAN AHEAD TODAY TO MINIMIZE YOUR STRESS TOMORROW.

(OR YOU CAN JUST WRITE OR DRAW SOMETHING SILLY DOWN BELOW AND GO TO BED SMILING.)

PLANS FOR TOMORROW/TO DO LIST:

CREATE YOUR OWN INSPIRING QUOTE AND SHARE YOUR WISDOM WITH OTHERS!

_____

_____

Date ___/___/20__

STRESSFUL MOMENTS:

_____

_____

HAPPY MOMENTS:

_____

_____

_____

Family Bonding Time…

-WRITE OR DRAW SOMETHING SILLY IN THE SPACE DOWN BELOW THAT WILL PUT A HUGE SMILE ON YOUR FACE. ALWAYS TRY TO GO TO BED SMILING AND FEELING HAPPY!

-THINK OF WAYS YOU CAN MAKE YOUR DAY EVEN BETTER TOMORROW.

-ALWAYS SHARE YOUR THOUGHTS AND CONCERNS (even when it is hard to do sometimes) WITH YOUR LOVING FAMILY FOR PROPER GUIDANCE AND GREAT IDEAS.

WRITE THEM DOWN BELOW IF NEEDED.

"The weak can never forgive. Forgiveness is the attribute of the strong."[1]
~Mahatma Gandhi

Date ___ / ___ /20__

STRESSFUL MOMENTS:

_____

_____

_____

HAPPY MOMENTS:

_____

_____

_____

PLAN AHEAD TODAY TO MINIMIZE YOUR STRESS TOMORROW.
(OR YOU CAN JUST WRITE OR DRAW SOMETHING SILLY DOWN BELOW AND GO TO BED SMILING.)
PLANS FOR TOMORROW/TO DO LIST:

CREATE YOUR OWN INSPIRING QUOTE AND SHARE YOUR WISDOM WITH OTHERS!

_____

_____

Date ___/___/20__

STRESSFUL MOMENTS:

_____

_____

HAPPY MOMENTS:

_____

_____

_____

Family Bonding Time...

-WRITE OR DRAW SOMETHING SILLY IN THE SPACE DOWN BELOW THAT WILL PUT A HUGE SMILE ON YOUR FACE. ALWAYS TRY TO GO TO BED SMILING AND FEELING HAPPY!

-THINK OF WAYS YOU CAN MAKE YOUR DAY EVEN BETTER TOMORROW.

-ALWAYS SHARE YOUR THOUGHTS AND CONCERNS (even when it is hard to do sometimes) WITH YOUR LOVING FAMILY FOR PROPER GUIDANCE AND GREAT IDEAS. WRITE THEM DOWN BELOW IF NEEDED.

"Live as if you were to die tomorrow. Learn as if you were to live forever."[1]
~Mahatma Gandhi

Date ___/___/20__

STRESSFUL MOMENTS:

_____

_____

_____

HAPPY MOMENTS:

_____

_____

_____

PLAN AHEAD TODAY TO MINIMIZE YOUR STRESS TOMORROW.
(OR YOU CAN JUST WRITE OR DRAW SOMETHING SILLY DOWN BELOW AND GO TO BED SMILING.)
PLANS FOR TOMORROW/TO DO LIST:

CREATE YOUR OWN INSPIRING QUOTE AND SHARE YOUR WISDOM WITH OTHERS!

_____

_____

Date ___/___/20__

STRESSFUL MOMENTS:

_____

_____

HAPPY MOMENTS:

_____

_____

Family Bonding Time…

-WRITE OR DRAW SOMETHING SILLY IN THE SPACE DOWN BELOW THAT WILL PUT A HUGE SMILE ON YOUR FACE. ALWAYS TRY TO GO TO BED SMILING AND FEELING HAPPY!

-THINK OF WAYS YOU CAN MAKE YOUR DAY EVEN BETTER TOMORROW.

-ALWAYS SHARE YOUR THOUGHTS AND CONCERNS (even when it is hard to do sometimes) WITH YOUR LOVING FAMILY FOR PROPER GUIDANCE AND GREAT IDEAS.

WRITE THEM DOWN BELOW IF NEEDED.

"It's a new day, fresh start, fresh energy, new opportunities. Get your mind right, be thankful, be positive and start your day right."(10)   ~unknown

Date ___/___/20__

STRESSFUL MOMENTS:

_____

_____

_____

HAPPY MOMENTS:

_____

_____

_____

PLAN AHEAD TODAY TO MINIMIZE YOUR STRESS TOMORROW.
(OR YOU CAN JUST WRITE OR DRAW SOMETHING SILLY DOWN BELOW AND GO TO BED SMILING.)
PLANS FOR TOMORROW/TO DO LIST:

CREATE YOUR **OWN** INSPIRING **QUOTE** AND **SHARE YOUR WISDOM** WITH OTHERS!

_____

_____

Date ___/___/20__

STRESSFUL MOMENTS:

_____

_____

HAPPY MOMENTS:

_____

_____

_____

Family Bonding Time...

-**WRITE OR DRAW SOMETHING SILLY IN THE SPACE DOWN BELOW THAT** WILL PUT A HUGE SMILE ON YOUR FACE. ALWAYS TRY TO GO TO BED SMILING AND FEELING HAPPY!

-**THINK** OF WAYS YOU CAN MAKE YOUR DAY EVEN BETTER TOMORROW.

-**ALWAYS SHARE** YOUR THOUGHTS AND CONCERNS (even when it is hard to do sometimes) WITH YOUR LOVING FAMILY FOR PROPER GUIDANCE AND GREAT IDEAS. WRITE THEM DOWN BELOW IF NEEDED.

"Attitude is a little thing that makes a big difference."(1)   ~W.Churchill

Date ___/___/20__

STRESSFUL MOMENTS:

_____

_____

_____

HAPPY MOMENTS:

_____

_____

_____

PLAN AHEAD TODAY TO MINIMIZE YOUR STRESS TOMORROW.
(OR YOU CAN JUST WRITE OR DRAW SOMETHING SILLY DOWN BELOW AND GO TO BED SMILING.)
PLANS FOR TOMORROW/TO DO LIST:

CREATE YOUR OWN INSPIRING QUOTE AND SHARE YOUR WISDOM WITH OTHERS!

_____

_____

Date ___/___/20__

STRESSFUL MOMENTS:

_____

_____

HAPPY MOMENTS:

_____

_____

Family Bonding Time...

-WRITE OR DRAW SOMETHING SILLY IN THE SPACE DOWN BELOW THAT WILL PUT A HUGE SMILE ON YOUR FACE. ALWAYS TRY TO GO TO BED SMILING AND FEELING HAPPY!
-THINK OF WAYS YOU CAN MAKE YOUR DAY EVEN BETTER TOMORROW.
-ALWAYS SHARE YOUR THOUGHTS AND CONCERNS (even when it is hard to do sometimes) WITH YOUR LOVING FAMILY FOR PROPER GUIDANCE AND GREAT IDEAS. WRITE THEM DOWN BELOW IF NEEDED.

"If your actions inspire others to dream more, learn more, do more and become more, you are a leader."[1]

~John Quincy Adams

Date ___/___/20__

STRESSFUL MOMENTS:

_____

_____

_____

HAPPY MOMENTS:

_____

_____

_____

PLAN AHEAD TODAY TO MINIMIZE YOUR STRESS TOMORROW.
(OR YOU CAN JUST WRITE OR DRAW SOMETHING SILLY DOWN BELOW AND GO TO BED SMILING.)
PLANS FOR TOMORROW/TO DO LIST:

CREATE YOUR **OWN** INSPIRING **QUOTE** AND **SHARE YOUR WISDOM**
WITH OTHERS!

_____

_____

Date ___/ ___/20__

STRESSFUL MOMENTS:

_____

_____

HAPPY MOMENTS:

_____

_____

Family Bonding Time...

-WRITE OR DRAW SOMETHING SILLY IN THE SPACE DOWN BELOW THAT WILL
PUT A HUGE SMILE ON YOUR FACE. ALWAYS TRY TO GO TO BED SMILING AND
FEELING HAPPY!
-THINK OF WAYS YOU CAN MAKE YOUR DAY EVEN BETTER TOMORROW.
-ALWAYS SHARE YOUR THOUGHTS AND CONCERNS (even when it is hard to do
sometimes) WITH YOUR LOVING FAMILY FOR PROPER GUIDANCE AND GREAT IDEAS.

WRITE THEM DOWN BELOW IF NEEDED.

"Start by doing what's necessary; then do what's possible; and suddenly you are doing the impossible."(1)

~St. Francis of Assisi

Date ___/___/20__

STRESSFUL MOMENTS:

_____

_____

_____

HAPPY MOMENTS:

_____

_____

_____

PLAN AHEAD TODAY TO MINIMIZE YOUR STRESS TOMORROW.
(OR YOU CAN JUST WRITE OR DRAW SOMETHING SILLY DOWN BELOW AND GO TO BED SMILING.)
PLANS FOR TOMORROW/TO DO LIST:

Believe You Can

"Nothing builds self-esteem and self-confidence like accomplishment."[1]
~Thomas Carlyle

Date ___ / ___ /20__

STRESSFUL MOMENTS:

_____

_____

_____

HAPPY MOMENTS:

_____

_____

_____

PLAN AHEAD TODAY TO MINIMIZE YOUR STRESS TOMORROW.
(OR YOU CAN JUST WRITE OR DRAW SOMETHING SILLY DOWN BELOW AND GO TO BED SMILING.)
PLANS FOR TOMORROW/TO DO LIST:

CREATE YOUR OWN INSPIRING QUOTE AND SHARE YOUR WISDOM WITH OTHERS!

_____

_____

Date ___/___/20__

STRESSFUL MOMENTS:

_____

_____

HAPPY MOMENTS:

_____

_____

_____

Family Bonding Time...

-WRITE OR DRAW SOMETHING SILLY IN THE SPACE DOWN BELOW THAT WILL PUT A HUGE SMILE ON YOUR FACE. ALWAYS TRY TO GO TO BED SMILING AND FEELING HAPPY!

-THINK OF WAYS YOU CAN MAKE YOUR DAY EVEN BETTER TOMORROW.

-ALWAYS SHARE YOUR THOUGHTS AND CONCERNS (even when it is hard to do sometimes) WITH YOUR LOVING FAMILY FOR PROPER GUIDANCE AND GREAT IDEAS.

WRITE THEM DOWN BELOW IF NEEDED.

"Teamwork is the fuel that allows common people to attain uncommon results."[1]

~Andrew Carnegie

Date ___/___/20__

STRESSFUL MOMENTS:

_____

_____

_____

HAPPY MOMENTS:

_____

_____

_____

PLAN AHEAD TODAY TO MINIMIZE YOUR STRESS TOMORROW.
(OR YOU CAN JUST WRITE OR DRAW SOMETHING SILLY DOWN BELOW AND GO TO BED SMILING.)

PLANS FOR TOMORROW/TO DO LIST:

CREATE YOUR OWN INSPIRING QUOTE AND SHARE YOUR WISDOM WITH OTHERS!

_____

_____

Date ___/___/20__

STRESSFUL MOMENTS:

_____

_____

HAPPY MOMENTS:

_____

_____

_____

Family Bonding Time...

-WRITE OR DRAW SOMETHING SILLY IN THE SPACE DOWN BELOW THAT WILL PUT A HUGE SMILE ON YOUR FACE. ALWAYS TRY TO GO TO BED SMILING AND FEELING HAPPY!

-THINK OF WAYS YOU CAN MAKE YOUR DAY EVEN BETTER TOMORROW.

-ALWAYS SHARE YOUR THOUGHTS AND CONCERNS (even when it is hard to do sometimes) WITH YOUR LOVING FAMILY FOR PROPER GUIDANCE AND GREAT IDEAS.

WRITE THEM DOWN BELOW IF NEEDED.

"Kindness is the oil that takes the friction out of life."(2)   ~unknown

Date ___/___/20___

STRESSFUL MOMENTS:

_____

_____

_____

HAPPY MOMENTS:

_____

_____

_____

PLAN AHEAD TODAY TO MINIMIZE YOUR STRESS TOMORROW.
(OR YOU CAN JUST WRITE OR DRAW SOMETHING SILLY DOWN BELOW AND GO TO
BED SMILING.)
PLANS FOR TOMORROW/TO DO LIST:

CREATE YOUR **OWN** INSPIRING **QUOTE** AND **SHARE YOUR WISDOM** WITH OTHERS!

_____

_____

Date ___/___/20__

STRESSFUL MOMENTS:

_____

_____

HAPPY MOMENTS:

_____

_____

_____

Family Bonding Time...

-**WRITE OR DRAW SOMETHING SILLY IN THE SPACE DOWN BELOW THAT** WILL PUT A HUGE SMILE ON YOUR FACE. ALWAYS TRY TO GO TO BED SMILING AND FEELING HAPPY!

-**THINK** OF WAYS YOU CAN MAKE YOUR DAY EVEN BETTER TOMORROW.

-**ALWAYS SHARE** YOUR THOUGHTS AND CONCERNS (even when it is hard to do sometimes) WITH YOUR LOVING FAMILY FOR PROPER GUIDANCE AND GREAT IDEAS.

WRITE THEM DOWN BELOW IF NEEDED.

Remember...family, real friends, and education ALWAYS come first! These are the people who will support you no matter what.

Date ___/___/20__

STRESSFUL MOMENTS:

_____

_____

_____

HAPPY MOMENTS:

_____

_____

_____

PLAN AHEAD TODAY TO MINIMIZE YOUR STRESS TOMORROW.
(OR YOU CAN JUST WRITE OR DRAW SOMETHING SILLY DOWN BELOW AND GO TO BED SMILING.)
PLANS FOR TOMORROW/TO DO LIST:

CREATE YOUR OWN INSPIRING QUOTE AND SHARE YOUR WISDOM WITH OTHERS!

_____

_____

Date ___/___/20__

STRESSFUL MOMENTS:

_____

_____

HAPPY MOMENTS:

_____

_____

_____

Family Bonding Time...

-WRITE OR DRAW SOMETHING SILLY IN THE SPACE DOWN BELOW THAT WILL PUT A HUGE SMILE ON YOUR FACE. ALWAYS TRY TO GO TO BED SMILING AND FEELING HAPPY!

-THINK OF WAYS YOU CAN MAKE YOUR DAY EVEN BETTER TOMORROW.

-ALWAYS SHARE YOUR THOUGHTS AND CONCERNS (even when it is hard to do sometimes) WITH YOUR LOVING FAMILY FOR PROPER GUIDANCE AND GREAT IDEAS.

WRITE THEM DOWN BELOW IF NEEDED.

"See Miracles In Life Every day !"(2)

~unknown

Date ___/___/20__

STRESSFUL MOMENTS:

_____

_____

_____

HAPPY MOMENTS:

_____

_____

_____

PLAN AHEAD TODAY TO MINIMIZE YOUR STRESS TOMORROW.
(OR YOU CAN JUST WRITE OR DRAW SOMETHING SILLY DOWN BELOW AND GO TO BED SMILING.)
PLANS FOR TOMORROW/TO DO LIST:

CREATE YOUR OWN INSPIRING QUOTE AND SHARE YOUR WISDOM WITH OTHERS!

_____

_____

Date ___/___/20___

STRESSFUL MOMENTS:

_____

_____

HAPPY MOMENTS:

_____

_____

Family Bonding Time...

-WRITE OR DRAW SOMETHING SILLY IN THE SPACE DOWN BELOW THAT WILL PUT A HUGE SMILE ON YOUR FACE. ALWAYS TRY TO GO TO BED SMILING AND FEELING HAPPY!

-THINK OF WAYS YOU CAN MAKE YOUR DAY EVEN BETTER TOMORROW.

-ALWAYS SHARE YOUR THOUGHTS AND CONCERNS (even when it is hard to do sometimes) WITH YOUR LOVING FAMILY FOR PROPER GUIDANCE AND GREAT IDEAS.

WRITE THEM DOWN BELOW IF NEEDED.

Date ___/___/20__

STRESSFUL MOMENTS:

_____

_____

_____

HAPPY MOMENTS:

_____

_____

_____

PLAN AHEAD TODAY TO MINIMIZE YOUR STRESS TOMORROW.
(OR YOU CAN JUST WRITE OR DRAW SOMETHING SILLY DOWN BELOW AND GO TO BED SMILING.)
PLANS FOR TOMORROW/TO DO LIST:

CREATE YOUR **OWN** INSPIRING **QUOTE** AND **SHARE YOUR WISDOM** WITH OTHERS!

_____

_____

Date ___/___/20__

STRESSFUL MOMENTS:

_____

_____

HAPPY MOMENTS:

_____

_____

_____

Family Bonding Time...

-WRITE OR DRAW SOMETHING SILLY IN THE SPACE DOWN BELOW THAT WILL PUT A HUGE SMILE ON YOUR FACE. ALWAYS TRY TO GO TO BED SMILING AND FEELING HAPPY!

-**THINK** OF WAYS YOU CAN MAKE YOUR DAY EVEN BETTER TOMORROW.

-**ALWAYS SHARE** YOUR THOUGHTS AND CONCERNS (even when it is hard to do sometimes) WITH YOUR LOVING FAMILY FOR PROPER GUIDANCE AND GREAT IDEAS. WRITE THEM DOWN BELOW IF NEEDED.

"Many people will walk in and out of your life, but only true friends will leave footprints in your heart."(1)

~Eleanor Roosevelt

Date ___/___/20__

STRESSFUL MOMENTS:

_____

_____

_____

HAPPY MOMENTS:

_____

_____

_____

PLAN AHEAD TODAY TO MINIMIZE YOUR STRESS TOMORROW.
(OR YOU CAN JUST WRITE OR DRAW SOMETHING SILLY DOWN BELOW AND GO TO BED SMILING.)

PLANS FOR TOMORROW/TO DO LIST:

Positive Positive Life Vibes

"Anyone who has never made a mistake has never tried anything new."[1]
~Albert Einstein

Date ___ / ___ /20__

STRESSFUL MOMENTS:

_____

_____

_____

HAPPY MOMENTS:

_____

_____

_____

PLAN AHEAD TODAY TO MINIMIZE YOUR STRESS TOMORROW.
(OR YOU CAN JUST WRITE OR DRAW SOMETHING SILLY DOWN BELOW AND GO TO BED SMILING.)
PLANS FOR TOMORROW/TO DO LIST:

CREATE YOUR OWN INSPIRING QUOTE AND SHARE YOUR WISDOM WITH OTHERS!

_____

_____

Date ___/___/20__

STRESSFUL MOMENTS:

_____

_____

HAPPY MOMENTS:

_____

_____

_____

Family Bonding Time...

-WRITE OR DRAW SOMETHING SILLY IN THE SPACE DOWN BELOW THAT WILL PUT A HUGE SMILE ON YOUR FACE. ALWAYS TRY TO GO TO BED SMILING AND FEELING HAPPY!

-THINK OF WAYS YOU CAN MAKE YOUR DAY EVEN BETTER TOMORROW.

-ALWAYS SHARE YOUR THOUGHTS AND CONCERNS (even when it is hard to do sometimes) WITH YOUR LOVING FAMILY FOR PROPER GUIDANCE AND GREAT IDEAS. WRITE THEM DOWN BELOW IF NEEDED.

"The true art of memory is the art of attention."(1)   ~Samuel Johnson

Date ___ / ___ /20__

STRESSFUL MOMENTS:

_____

_____

_____

HAPPY MOMENTS:

_____

_____

_____

PLAN AHEAD TODAY TO MINIMIZE YOUR STRESS TOMORROW.
(OR YOU CAN JUST WRITE OR DRAW SOMETHING SILLY DOWN BELOW AND GO TO
BED SMILING.)
PLANS FOR TOMORROW/TO DO LIST:

CREATE YOUR OWN INSPIRING QUOTE AND SHARE YOUR WISDOM WITH OTHERS!

_____

_____

Date ___/___/20__

STRESSFUL MOMENTS:

_____

_____

HAPPY MOMENTS:

_____

_____

_____

Family Bonding Time...

-WRITE OR DRAW SOMETHING SILLY IN THE SPACE DOWN BELOW THAT WILL PUT A HUGE SMILE ON YOUR FACE. ALWAYS TRY TO GO TO BED SMILING AND FEELING HAPPY!   -THINK OF WAYS YOU CAN MAKE YOUR DAY EVEN BETTER TOMORROW.

-ALWAYS SHARE YOUR THOUGHTS AND CONCERNS (even when it is hard to do sometimes) WITH YOUR LOVING FAMILY FOR PROPER GUIDANCE AND GREAT IDEAS.

WRITE THEM DOWN BELOW IF NEEDED.

"It is not a mistake to turn back, if you are on the wrong road."(2)
~unknown

Date ___/___/20__

STRESSFUL MOMENTS:

_____

_____

_____

HAPPY MOMENTS:

_____

_____

_____

PLAN AHEAD TODAY TO MINIMIZE YOUR STRESS TOMORROW.
(OR YOU CAN JUST WRITE OR DRAW SOMETHING SILLY DOWN BELOW AND GO TO BED SMILING.)
PLANS FOR TOMORROW/TO DO LIST:

CREATE YOUR **OWN** INSPIRING **QUOTE** AND **SHARE YOUR WISDOM** WITH OTHERS!

_____

_____

Date ___/___/20__

STRESSFUL MOMENTS:

_____

_____

HAPPY MOMENTS:

_____

_____

Family Bonding Time...

-WRITE OR DRAW SOMETHING SILLY IN THE SPACE DOWN BELOW THAT WILL PUT A HUGE SMILE ON YOUR FACE. ALWAYS TRY TO GO TO BED SMILING AND FEELING HAPPY!

-THINK OF WAYS YOU CAN MAKE YOUR DAY EVEN BETTER TOMORROW.

-ALWAYS SHARE YOUR THOUGHTS AND CONCERNS (even when it is hard to do sometimes) WITH YOUR LOVING FAMILY FOR PROPER GUIDANCE AND GREAT IDEAS.

WRITE THEM DOWN BELOW IF NEEDED.

"Some pursue happiness...others create it."(2)   ~unknown

Date ___/___/20__

STRESSFUL MOMENTS:

_____

_____

_____

HAPPY MOMENTS:

_____

_____

_____

PLAN AHEAD TODAY TO MINIMIZE YOUR STRESS TOMORROW.
(OR YOU CAN JUST WRITE OR DRAW SOMETHING SILLY DOWN BELOW AND GO TO BED SMILING.)
PLANS FOR TOMORROW/TO DO LIST:

CREATE YOUR **OWN** INSPIRING **QUOTE** AND **SHARE YOUR WISDOM**
WITH OTHERS!

_____

_____

Date ___/___/20__

STRESSFUL MOMENTS:

_____

_____

HAPPY MOMENTS:

_____

_____

Family Bonding Time...

-WRITE OR DRAW SOMETHING SILLY IN THE SPACE DOWN BELOW THAT WILL
PUT A HUGE SMILE ON YOUR FACE. ALWAYS TRY TO GO TO BED SMILING AND
FEELING HAPPY!
-THINK OF WAYS YOU CAN MAKE YOUR DAY EVEN BETTER TOMORROW.
-ALWAYS SHARE YOUR THOUGHTS AND CONCERNS (even when it is hard to do
sometimes) WITH YOUR LOVING FAMILY FOR PROPER GUIDANCE AND GREAT IDEAS.
WRITE THEM DOWN BELOW IF NEEDED.

"There are no great limits to growth because there are no limits of human intelligence, imagination, and wonder."(1)

~Ronald Reagan

Date ___/___/20__

STRESSFUL MOMENTS:

_____

_____

_____

HAPPY MOMENTS:

_____

_____

_____

PLAN AHEAD TODAY TO MINIMIZE YOUR STRESS TOMORROW.
(OR YOU CAN JUST WRITE OR DRAW SOMETHING SILLY DOWN BELOW AND GO TO BED SMILING.)
PLANS FOR TOMORROW/TO DO LIST:

CREATE YOUR OWN INSPIRING QUOTE AND SHARE YOUR WISDOM WITH OTHERS!

_____

_____

Date ___/___/20__

STRESSFUL MOMENTS:

_____

_____

HAPPY MOMENTS:

_____

_____

Family Bonding Time...

-WRITE OR DRAW SOMETHING SILLY IN THE SPACE DOWN BELOW THAT WILL PUT A HUGE SMILE ON YOUR FACE. ALWAYS TRY TO GO TO BED SMILING AND FEELING HAPPY!

-THINK OF WAYS YOU CAN MAKE YOUR DAY EVEN BETTER TOMORROW.

-ALWAYS SHARE YOUR THOUGHTS AND CONCERNS (even when it is hard to do sometimes) WITH YOUR LOVING FAMILY FOR PROPER GUIDANCE AND GREAT IDEAS.

WRITE THEM DOWN BELOW IF NEEDED.

"Efforts and courage are not enough without purpose and direction."[1]

~John F. Kennedy

Date ___/___/20__

STRESSFUL MOMENTS:

_____

_____

_____

HAPPY MOMENTS:

_____

_____

_____

PLAN AHEAD TODAY TO MINIMIZE YOUR STRESS TOMORROW.
(OR YOU CAN JUST WRITE OR DRAW SOMETHING SILLY DOWN BELOW AND GO TO BED SMILING.)
PLANS FOR TOMORROW/TO DO LIST:

CREATE YOUR OWN INSPIRING QUOTE AND SHARE YOUR WISDOM WITH OTHERS!

_____

_____

Date ___/___/20__

STRESSFUL MOMENTS:

_____

_____

HAPPY MOMENTS:

_____

_____

Family Bonding Time...

-WRITE OR DRAW SOMETHING SILLY IN THE SPACE DOWN BELOW THAT WILL PUT A HUGE SMILE ON YOUR FACE. ALWAYS TRY TO GO TO BED SMILING AND FEELING HAPPY!

-THINK OF WAYS YOU CAN MAKE YOUR DAY EVEN BETTER TOMORROW.

-ALWAYS SHARE YOUR THOUGHTS AND CONCERNS (even when it is hard to do sometimes) WITH YOUR LOVING FAMILY FOR PROPER GUIDANCE AND GREAT IDEAS. WRITE THEM DOWN BELOW IF NEEDED.

"Do not waste time dreaming of great faraway opportunities; do the best you can where you are."(1)

~O.S.Marden

Date ___/___/20__

STRESSFUL MOMENTS:

_____

_____

_____

HAPPY MOMENTS:

_____

_____

_____

PLAN AHEAD TODAY TO MINIMIZE YOUR STRESS TOMORROW.
(OR YOU CAN JUST WRITE OR DRAW SOMETHING SILLY DOWN BELOW AND GO TO BED SMILING.)
PLANS FOR TOMORROW/TO DO LIST:

CREATE YOUR **OWN** INSPIRING **QUOTE** AND **SHARE YOUR WISDOM** WITH OTHERS!

_____

_____

Date ___/___/20__

STRESSFUL MOMENTS:

_____

_____

HAPPY MOMENTS:

_____

_____

Family Bonding Time...

-**WRITE OR DRAW SOMETHING SILLY IN THE SPACE DOWN BELOW THAT** WILL PUT A HUGE SMILE ON YOUR FACE. ALWAYS TRY TO GO TO BED SMILING AND FEELING HAPPY!

-**THINK** OF WAYS YOU CAN MAKE YOUR DAY EVEN BETTER TOMORROW.

-**ALWAYS SHARE** YOUR THOUGHTS AND CONCERNS (even when it is hard to do sometimes) WITH YOUR LOVING FAMILY FOR PROPER GUIDANCE AND GREAT IDEAS.

WRITE THEM DOWN BELOW IF NEEDED.

"Life is like riding a bicycle. To keep your balance you must keep moving."(1)

~Albert Einstein

Date ___/___/20__

STRESSFUL MOMENTS:

_____

_____

_____

HAPPY MOMENTS:

_____

_____

_____

PLAN AHEAD TODAY TO MINIMIZE YOUR STRESS TOMORROW.
(OR YOU CAN JUST WRITE OR DRAW SOMETHING SILLY DOWN BELOW AND GO TO BED SMILING.)
PLANS FOR TOMORROW/TO DO LIST:

"Don't let anyone steal your happiness...because it wasn't theirs to begin with."(2)

~unknown

Date ___/___/20__

STRESSFUL MOMENTS:

_____

_____

_____

HAPPY MOMENTS:

_____

_____

_____

PLAN AHEAD TODAY TO MINIMIZE YOUR STRESS TOMORROW.

(OR YOU CAN JUST WRITE OR DRAW SOMETHING SILLY DOWN BELOW AND GO TO BED SMILING.)

PLANS FOR TOMORROW/TO DO LIST:

CREATE YOUR **OWN** INSPIRING **QUOTE** AND **SHARE YOUR WISDOM** WITH OTHERS!

_____

_____

Date ___/___/20__

STRESSFUL MOMENTS:

_____

_____

HAPPY MOMENTS:

_____

_____

_____

Family Bonding Time...

-WRITE OR DRAW SOMETHING SILLY IN THE SPACE DOWN BELOW THAT WILL PUT A HUGE SMILE ON YOUR FACE. ALWAYS TRY TO GO TO BED SMILING AND FEELING HAPPY!

-THINK OF WAYS YOU CAN MAKE YOUR DAY EVEN BETTER TOMORROW.

-ALWAYS SHARE YOUR THOUGHTS AND CONCERNS (even when it is hard to do sometimes) WITH YOUR LOVING FAMILY FOR PROPER GUIDANCE AND GREAT IDEAS. WRITE THEM DOWN BELOW IF NEEDED.

"Everything happens for a reason... Live it. Love it. Learn from it."(2)

~unknown

Date ___/___/20__

STRESSFUL MOMENTS:

_____

_____

_____

HAPPY MOMENTS:

_____

_____

_____

PLAN AHEAD TODAY TO MINIMIZE YOUR STRESS TOMORROW.
(OR YOU CAN JUST WRITE OR DRAW SOMETHING SILLY DOWN BELOW AND GO TO BED SMILING.)
PLANS FOR TOMORROW/TO DO LIST:

CREATE YOUR OWN INSPIRING QUOTE AND SHARE YOUR WISDOM WITH OTHERS!

_____

_____

Date ___/___/20___

STRESSFUL MOMENTS:

_____

_____

HAPPY MOMENTS:

_____

_____

Family Bonding Time...

-WRITE OR DRAW SOMETHING SILLY IN THE SPACE DOWN BELOW THAT WILL PUT A HUGE SMILE ON YOUR FACE. ALWAYS TRY TO GO TO BED SMILING AND FEELING HAPPY!

-THINK OF WAYS YOU CAN MAKE YOUR DAY EVEN BETTER TOMORROW.

-ALWAYS SHARE YOUR THOUGHTS AND CONCERNS (even when it is hard to do sometimes) WITH YOUR LOVING FAMILY FOR PROPER GUIDANCE AND GREAT IDEAS. WRITE THEM DOWN BELOW IF NEEDED.

"Inner peace begins the moment you choose not to allow another person or event to control your emotions."(2)

~unknown

Date ___/___/20__

STRESSFUL MOMENTS:

_____

_____

_____

HAPPY MOMENTS:

_____

_____

_____

PLAN AHEAD TODAY TO MINIMIZE YOUR STRESS TOMORROW.
(OR YOU CAN JUST WRITE OR DRAW SOMETHING SILLY DOWN BELOW AND GO TO BED SMILING.)
PLANS FOR TOMORROW/TO DO LIST:

CREATE YOUR **OWN** INSPIRING **QUOTE** AND **SHARE YOUR WISDOM**
WITH OTHERS!

_____

_____

Date ___/___/20__

STRESSFUL MOMENTS:

_____

_____

HAPPY MOMENTS:

_____

_____

Family Bonding Time...

-WRITE OR DRAW SOMETHING SILLY IN THE SPACE DOWN BELOW THAT WILL
PUT A HUGE SMILE ON YOUR FACE. ALWAYS TRY TO GO TO BED SMILING AND
FEELING HAPPY!
-THINK OF WAYS YOU CAN MAKE YOUR DAY EVEN BETTER TOMORROW.
-ALWAYS SHARE YOUR THOUGHTS AND CONCERNS (even when it is hard to do
sometimes) WITH YOUR LOVING FAMILY FOR PROPER GUIDANCE AND GREAT IDEAS.
WRITE THEM DOWN BELOW IF NEEDED.

"Everything in your life is a reflection of a choice you have made. If you want a different result, make a different choice."(2)   ~unknown

Date ___ / ___ /20___

STRESSFUL MOMENTS:

_____

_____

_____

HAPPY MOMENTS:

_____

_____

_____

PLAN AHEAD TODAY TO MINIMIZE YOUR STRESS TOMORROW.
(OR YOU CAN JUST WRITE OR DRAW SOMETHING SILLY DOWN BELOW AND GO TO BED SMILING.)
PLANS FOR TOMORROW/TO DO LIST:

CREATE your OWN inspiring QUOTE and SHARE YOUR WISDOM WITH OTHERS!

_____

_____

Date ___/___/20___

STRESSFUL MOMENTS:

_____

_____

HAPPY MOMENTS:

_____

_____

_____

Family Bonding Time...

-WRITE OR DRAW SOMETHING SILLY IN THE SPACE DOWN BELOW THAT WILL PUT A HUGE SMILE ON YOUR FACE. ALWAYS TRY TO GO TO BED SMILING AND FEELING HAPPY!

-THINK OF WAYS YOU CAN MAKE YOUR DAY EVEN BETTER TOMORROW.

-ALWAYS SHARE YOUR THOUGHTS AND CONCERNS (even when it is hard to do sometimes) WITH YOUR LOVING FAMILY FOR PROPER GUIDANCE AND GREAT IDEAS.

WRITE THEM DOWN BELOW IF NEEDED.

"Everyone you meet is fighting a battle that you know nothing about. Be kind. Always."(2)

Date ___/___/20__

STRESSFUL MOMENTS:

_____

_____

_____

HAPPY MOMENTS:

_____

_____

_____

PLAN AHEAD TODAY TO MINIMIZE YOUR STRESS TOMORROW.
(OR YOU CAN JUST WRITE OR DRAW SOMETHING SILLY DOWN BELOW AND GO TO BED SMILING.)
PLANS FOR TOMORROW/TO DO LIST:

CREATE YOUR OWN INSPIRING QUOTE AND SHARE YOUR WISDOM WITH OTHERS!

_____

_____

Date ___/___/20___

STRESSFUL MOMENTS:

_____

_____

HAPPY MOMENTS:

_____

_____

_____

Family Bonding Time...

-WRITE OR DRAW SOMETHING SILLY IN THE SPACE DOWN BELOW THAT WILL PUT A HUGE SMILE ON YOUR FACE. ALWAYS TRY TO GO TO BED SMILING AND FEELING HAPPY!

-THINK OF WAYS YOU CAN MAKE YOUR DAY EVEN BETTER TOMORROW.

-ALWAYS SHARE YOUR THOUGHTS AND CONCERNS (even when it is hard to do sometimes) WITH YOUR LOVING FAMILY FOR PROPER GUIDANCE AND GREAT IDEAS.

WRITE THEM DOWN BELOW IF NEEDED.

"Don't ruin a good day by thinking about a bad yesterday... Let it go!"(2)

~unknown

Date ___/___/20__

STRESSFUL MOMENTS:

_____

_____

_____

HAPPY MOMENTS:

_____

_____

_____

PLAN AHEAD TODAY TO MINIMIZE YOUR STRESS TOMORROW.
(OR YOU CAN JUST WRITE OR DRAW SOMETHING SILLY DOWN BELOW AND GO TO
BED SMILING.)
PLANS FOR TOMORROW/TO DO LIST:

CREATE YOUR OWN INSPIRING QUOTE AND SHARE YOUR WISDOM WITH OTHERS!

_____

_____

Date ___/___/20__

STRESSFUL MOMENTS:

_____

_____

HAPPY MOMENTS:

_____

_____

Family Bonding Time...

-WRITE OR DRAW SOMETHING SILLY IN THE SPACE DOWN BELOW THAT WILL PUT A HUGE SMILE ON YOUR FACE. ALWAYS TRY TO GO TO BED SMILING AND FEELING HAPPY!

-THINK OF WAYS YOU CAN MAKE YOUR DAY EVEN BETTER TOMORROW.

-ALWAYS SHARE YOUR THOUGHTS AND CONCERNS (even when it is hard to do sometimes) WITH YOUR LOVING FAMILY FOR PROPER GUIDANCE AND GREAT IDEAS.

WRITE THEM DOWN BELOW IF NEEDED.

"Don't change so people will like you. Be yourself, and the right people will love the real you."(2)

~unknown

Date ___/___/20__

STRESSFUL MOMENTS:

_____

_____

_____

HAPPY MOMENTS:

_____

_____

_____

PLAN AHEAD TODAY TO MINIMIZE YOUR STRESS TOMORROW.

(OR YOU CAN JUST WRITE OR DRAW SOMETHING SILLY DOWN BELOW AND GO TO BED SMILING.)

PLANS FOR TOMORROW/TO DO LIST:

Do
all
things
with
LOVE!

"Create a life that feels good on the inside, not one that just looks good on the outside."(2)

~unknown

Date ___/___/20__

STRESSFUL MOMENTS:

_____

_____

_____

HAPPY MOMENTS:

_____

_____

_____

PLAN AHEAD TODAY TO MINIMIZE YOUR STRESS TOMORROW.
(OR YOU CAN JUST WRITE OR DRAW SOMETHING SILLY DOWN BELOW AND GO TO BED SMILING.)
PLANS FOR TOMORROW/TO DO LIST:

CREATE your **OWN** inspiring **QUOTE** and **SHARE YOUR WISDOM** WITH OTHERS!

_____

_____

Date ___/___/20__

STRESSFUL MOMENTS:

_____

_____

HAPPY MOMENTS:

_____

_____

Family Bonding Time...

-WRITE OR DRAW SOMETHING SILLY IN THE SPACE DOWN BELOW THAT WILL PUT A HUGE SMILE ON YOUR FACE. ALWAYS TRY TO GO TO BED SMILING AND FEELING HAPPY!

-THINK OF WAYS YOU CAN MAKE YOUR DAY EVEN BETTER TOMORROW.

-ALWAYS SHARE YOUR THOUGHTS AND CONCERNS (even when it is hard to do sometimes) WITH YOUR LOVING FAMILY FOR PROPER GUIDANCE AND GREAT IDEAS.

WRITE THEM DOWN BELOW IF NEEDED.

Date ___/___/20__

STRESSFUL MOMENTS:

_____

_____

_____

HAPPY MOMENTS:

_____

_____

_____

PLAN AHEAD TODAY TO MINIMIZE YOUR STRESS TOMORROW.
(OR YOU CAN JUST WRITE OR DRAW SOMETHING SILLY DOWN BELOW AND GO TO
BED SMILING.)
PLANS FOR TOMORROW/TO DO LIST:

CREATE YOUR OWN INSPIRING QUOTE AND SHARE YOUR WISDOM WITH OTHERS!

_____

_____

Date ___/___/20__

STRESSFUL MOMENTS:

_____

_____

HAPPY MOMENTS:

_____

_____

Family Bonding Time...

-WRITE OR DRAW SOMETHING SILLY IN THE SPACE DOWN BELOW THAT WILL PUT A HUGE SMILE ON YOUR FACE. ALWAYS TRY TO GO TO BED SMILING AND FEELING HAPPY!

-THINK OF WAYS YOU CAN MAKE YOUR DAY EVEN BETTER TOMORROW.

-ALWAYS SHARE YOUR THOUGHTS AND CONCERNS (even when it is hard to do sometimes) WITH YOUR LOVING FAMILY FOR PROPER GUIDANCE AND GREAT IDEAS. WRITE THEM DOWN BELOW IF NEEDED.

"Appreciate your loved ones while you can, because none of us are going to be here forever."(2)

~unknown

Date ___/___/20__

STRESSFUL MOMENTS:

_____

_____

_____

HAPPY MOMENTS:

_____

_____

_____

PLAN AHEAD TODAY TO MINIMIZE YOUR STRESS TOMORROW.
(OR YOU CAN JUST WRITE OR DRAW SOMETHING SILLY DOWN BELOW AND GO TO BED SMILING.)
PLANS FOR TOMORROW/TO DO LIST:

CREATE YOUR OWN INSPIRING QUOTE AND SHARE YOUR WISDOM WITH OTHERS!

_____

_____

Date ___/___/20___

STRESSFUL MOMENTS:

_____

_____

HAPPY MOMENTS:

_____

_____

Family Bonding Time...

-WRITE OR DRAW SOMETHING SILLY IN THE SPACE DOWN BELOW THAT WILL PUT A HUGE SMILE ON YOUR FACE. ALWAYS TRY TO GO TO BED SMILING AND FEELING HAPPY!

-THINK OF WAYS YOU CAN MAKE YOUR DAY EVEN BETTER TOMORROW.

-ALWAYS SHARE YOUR THOUGHTS AND CONCERNS (even when it is hard to do sometimes) WITH YOUR LOVING FAMILY FOR PROPER GUIDANCE AND GREAT IDEAS. WRITE THEM DOWN BELOW IF NEEDED.

"ALWAYS believe that something wonderful is going to happen."(2)

~unknown

Date ___/___/20__

STRESSFUL MOMENTS:

_____

_____

_____

HAPPY MOMENTS:

_____

_____

_____

PLAN AHEAD TODAY TO MINIMIZE YOUR STRESS TOMORROW.
(OR YOU CAN JUST WRITE OR DRAW SOMETHING SILLY DOWN BELOW AND GO TO BED SMILING.)
PLANS FOR TOMORROW/TO DO LIST:

CREATE YOUR OWN INSPIRING QUOTE AND SHARE YOUR WISDOM WITH OTHERS!

_____

_____

Date ___/___/20__

STRESSFUL MOMENTS:

_____

_____

HAPPY MOMENTS:

_____

_____

Family Bonding Time...

-WRITE OR DRAW SOMETHING SILLY IN THE SPACE DOWN BELOW THAT WILL PUT A HUGE SMILE ON YOUR FACE. ALWAYS TRY TO GO TO BED SMILING AND FEELING HAPPY!

-THINK OF WAYS YOU CAN MAKE YOUR DAY EVEN BETTER TOMORROW.

-ALWAYS SHARE YOUR THOUGHTS AND CONCERNS (even when it is hard to do sometimes) WITH YOUR LOVING FAMILY FOR PROPER GUIDANCE AND GREAT IDEAS. WRITE THEM DOWN BELOW IF NEEDED.

Date ___/___/20__

STRESSFUL MOMENTS:

_____

_____

_____

HAPPY MOMENTS:

_____

_____

_____

PLAN AHEAD TODAY TO MINIMIZE YOUR STRESS TOMORROW.
(OR YOU CAN JUST WRITE OR DRAW SOMETHING SILLY DOWN BELOW AND GO TO
BED SMILING.)
PLANS FOR TOMORROW/TO DO LIST:

CREATE YOUR **OWN** INSPIRING **QUOTE** AND **SHARE YOUR WISDOM**
WITH OTHERS!

_____

_____

Date ___/___/20__

STRESSFUL MOMENTS:

_____

_____

HAPPY MOMENTS:

_____

_____

Family Bonding Time...

-**WRITE OR DRAW SOMETHING SILLY IN THE SPACE DOWN BELOW THAT** WILL
PUT A HUGE SMILE ON YOUR FACE. ALWAYS TRY TO GO TO BED SMILING AND
FEELING HAPPY!
-**THINK** OF WAYS YOU CAN MAKE YOUR DAY EVEN BETTER TOMORROW.
-**ALWAYS SHARE** YOUR THOUGHTS AND CONCERNS (even when it is hard to do
sometimes) WITH YOUR LOVING FAMILY FOR PROPER GUIDANCE AND GREAT IDEAS.
WRITE THEM DOWN BELOW IF NEEDED.

"The smile on my face doesn't mean my life is perfect. It means I appreciate all that I have been blessed with."(2)

~unknown

Date ___/___/20__

STRESSFUL MOMENTS:

_____

_____

_____

HAPPY MOMENTS:

_____

_____

_____

PLAN AHEAD TODAY TO MINIMIZE YOUR STRESS TOMORROW.

(OR YOU CAN JUST WRITE OR DRAW SOMETHING SILLY DOWN BELOW AND GO TO BED SMILING.)

PLANS FOR TOMORROW/TO DO LIST:

CREATE YOUR **OWN** INSPIRING **QUOTE** AND **SHARE YOUR WISDOM** WITH OTHERS!

_____

_____

Date ___/___/20__

STRESSFUL MOMENTS:

_____

_____

HAPPY MOMENTS:

_____

_____

Family Bonding Time...

-**WRITE OR DRAW SOMETHING SILLY IN THE SPACE DOWN BELOW THAT** WILL PUT A HUGE SMILE ON YOUR FACE. ALWAYS TRY TO GO TO BED SMILING AND FEELING HAPPY!

-**THINK** OF WAYS YOU CAN MAKE YOUR DAY EVEN BETTER TOMORROW.

-**ALWAYS SHARE** YOUR THOUGHTS AND CONCERNS (even when it is hard to do sometimes) WITH YOUR LOVING FAMILY FOR PROPER GUIDANCE AND GREAT IDEAS.

WRITE THEM DOWN BELOW IF NEEDED.

"Don't compare or compete... Be unique."(2)   ~unknown

Date ___/___/20__

STRESSFUL MOMENTS:

_____

_____

_____

HAPPY MOMENTS:

_____

_____

_____

PLAN AHEAD TODAY TO MINIMIZE YOUR STRESS TOMORROW.
(OR YOU CAN JUST WRITE OR DRAW SOMETHING SILLY DOWN BELOW AND GO TO BED SMILING.)
PLANS FOR TOMORROW/TO DO LIST:

CREATE YOUR OWN INSPIRING QUOTE AND SHARE YOUR WISDOM WITH OTHERS!

_____

_____

Date ___/___/20__

STRESSFUL MOMENTS:

_____

_____

HAPPY MOMENTS:

_____

_____

Family Bonding Time...

-WRITE OR DRAW SOMETHING SILLY IN THE SPACE DOWN BELOW THAT WILL PUT A HUGE SMILE ON YOUR FACE. ALWAYS TRY TO GO TO BED SMILING AND HAPPY! -THINK OF WAYS YOU CAN MAKE YOUR DAY EVEN BETTER TOMORROW. -ALWAYS SHARE YOUR THOUGHTS AND CONCERNS (even when it is hard to do sometimes) WITH YOUR LOVING FAMILY FOR PROPER GUIDANCE AND GREAT IDEAS.

WRITE THEM DOWN BELOW IF NEEDED.

"A little preparation saves a lot of frustration."(2)   ~unknown

Date ___/___/20__

STRESSFUL MOMENTS:

_____

_____

_____

HAPPY MOMENTS:

_____

_____

_____

PLAN AHEAD TODAY TO MINIMIZE YOUR STRESS TOMORROW.

(OR YOU CAN JUST WRITE OR DRAW SOMETHING SILLY DOWN BELOW AND GO TO BED SMILING.)

PLANS FOR TOMORROW/TO DO LIST:

LEARN
SOMETHING
NEW
TODAY

"Behavior is the mirror in which everyone shows their image."[1]

~Wolfgang Von Goeth

Date ___/___/20___

STRESSFUL MOMENTS:

_____

_____

_____

HAPPY MOMENTS:

_____

_____

_____

PLAN AHEAD TODAY TO MINIMIZE YOUR STRESS TOMORROW.
(OR YOU CAN JUST WRITE OR DRAW SOMETHING SILLY DOWN BELOW AND GO TO BED SMILING.)
PLANS FOR TOMORROW/TO DO LIST:

CREATE YOUR **OWN** INSPIRING **QUOTE** AND **SHARE YOUR WISDOM WITH OTHERS!**

_____

_____

Date ___ / ___ /20 __

STRESSFUL MOMENTS:

_____

_____

HAPPY MOMENTS:

_____

_____

_____

Family Bonding Time...

-WRITE OR DRAW SOMETHING SILLY IN THE SPACE DOWN BELOW THAT WILL PUT A HUGE SMILE ON YOUR FACE. ALWAYS TRY TO GO TO BED SMILING AND FEELING HAPPY!

-THINK OF WAYS YOU CAN MAKE YOUR DAY EVEN BETTER TOMORROW.

-ALWAYS SHARE YOUR THOUGHTS AND CONCERNS (even when it is hard to do sometimes) WITH YOUR LOVING FAMILY FOR PROPER GUIDANCE AND GREAT IDEAS. WRITE THEM DOWN BELOW IF NEEDED.

"Don't get caught up in what you can't control. Focus on the positive."(2)

~unknown

Date ___/___/20__

STRESSFUL MOMENTS:

_____

_____

_____

HAPPY MOMENTS:

_____

_____

_____

PLAN AHEAD TODAY TO MINIMIZE YOUR STRESS TOMORROW.
(OR YOU CAN JUST WRITE OR DRAW SOMETHING SILLY DOWN BELOW AND GO TO
BED SMILING.)
PLANS FOR TOMORROW/TO DO LIST:

CREATE YOUR **OWN** INSPIRING **QUOTE** AND **SHARE YOUR WISDOM** WITH OTHERS!

_____

_____

Date ___/___/20__

STRESSFUL MOMENTS:

_____

_____

HAPPY MOMENTS:

_____

_____

Family Bonding Time...

-WRITE OR DRAW SOMETHING SILLY IN THE SPACE DOWN BELOW THAT WILL PUT A HUGE SMILE ON YOUR FACE. ALWAYS TRY TO GO TO BED SMILING AND FEELING HAPPY!

-THINK OF WAYS YOU CAN MAKE YOUR DAY EVEN BETTER TOMORROW.

-ALWAYS SHARE YOUR THOUGHTS AND CONCERNS (even when it is hard to do sometimes) WITH YOUR LOVING FAMILY FOR PROPER GUIDANCE AND GREAT IDEAS.

WRITE THEM DOWN BELOW IF NEEDED.

"Self-control will give you unlimited control."(2)   ~unknown

Date ___/___/20__

STRESSFUL MOMENTS:

_____

_____

_____

HAPPY MOMENTS:

_____

_____

_____

PLAN AHEAD TODAY TO MINIMIZE YOUR STRESS TOMORROW.
(OR YOU CAN JUST WRITE OR DRAW SOMETHING SILLY DOWN BELOW AND GO TO BED SMILING.)
PLANS FOR TOMORROW/TO DO LIST:

CREATE YOUR OWN INSPIRING QUOTE AND SHARE YOUR WISDOM WITH OTHERS!

_____

_____

Date ___/___/20__

STRESSFUL MOMENTS:

_____

_____

HAPPY MOMENTS:

_____

_____

Family Bonding Time...

-WRITE OR DRAW SOMETHING SILLY IN THE SPACE DOWN BELOW THAT WILL PUT A HUGE SMILE ON YOUR FACE. ALWAYS TRY TO GO TO BED SMILING AND FEELING HAPPY!

-THINK OF WAYS YOU CAN MAKE YOUR DAY EVEN BETTER TOMORROW.

-ALWAYS SHARE YOUR THOUGHTS AND CONCERNS (even when it is hard to do sometimes) WITH YOUR LOVING FAMILY FOR PROPER GUIDANCE AND GREAT IDEAS.

WRITE THEM DOWN BELOW IF NEEDED.

"There is no pillow so soft as a clear conscience."(2)   ~unknown

Date ___/___/20__

STRESSFUL MOMENTS:

_____

_____

_____

HAPPY MOMENTS:

_____

_____

_____

PLAN AHEAD TODAY TO MINIMIZE YOUR STRESS TOMORROW.
(OR YOU CAN JUST WRITE OR DRAW SOMETHING SILLY DOWN BELOW AND GO TO
BED SMILING.)
PLANS FOR TOMORROW/TO DO LIST:

CREATE YOUR OWN INSPIRING QUOTE AND SHARE YOUR WISDOM WITH OTHERS!

_____

_____

Date ___/___/20__

STRESSFUL MOMENTS:

_____

_____

HAPPY MOMENTS:

_____

_____

Family Bonding Time...

-WRITE OR DRAW SOMETHING SILLY IN THE SPACE DOWN BELOW THAT WILL PUT A HUGE SMILE ON YOUR FACE. ALWAYS TRY TO GO TO BED SMILING AND FEELING HAPPY!

-THINK OF WAYS YOU CAN MAKE YOUR DAY EVEN BETTER TOMORROW.

-ALWAYS SHARE YOUR THOUGHTS AND CONCERNS (even when it is hard to do sometimes) WITH YOUR LOVING FAMILY FOR PROPER GUIDANCE AND GREAT IDEAS.

WRITE THEM DOWN BELOW IF NEEDED.

"Do what makes *you* happy. Be with who makes *you* smile.
Laugh as much as *you* breathe and love as long as *you* live."(2)   ~unknown

Date ___/___/20__

STRESSFUL MOMENTS:

_____

_____

_____

HAPPY MOMENTS:

_____

_____

_____

PLAN AHEAD TODAY TO MINIMIZE YOUR STRESS TOMORROW.
(OR YOU CAN JUST WRITE OR DRAW SOMETHING SILLY DOWN BELOW AND GO TO BED SMILING.)
PLANS FOR TOMORROW/TO DO LIST:

CREATE YOUR **OWN** INSPIRING **QUOTE** AND **SHARE YOUR WISDOM** WITH OTHERS!

_____

_____

Date ___/___/20__

STRESSFUL MOMENTS:

_____

_____

HAPPY MOMENTS:

_____

_____

Family Bonding Time...

-WRITE OR DRAW SOMETHING SILLY IN THE SPACE DOWN BELOW THAT WILL PUT A HUGE SMILE ON YOUR FACE. ALWAYS TRY TO GO TO BED SMILING AND FEELING HAPPY!

-THINK OF WAYS YOU CAN MAKE YOUR DAY EVEN BETTER TOMORROW.

-ALWAYS SHARE YOUR THOUGHTS AND CONCERNS (even when it is hard to do sometimes) WITH YOUR LOVING FAMILY FOR PROPER GUIDANCE AND GREAT IDEAS.

WRITE THEM DOWN BELOW IF NEEDED.

"Condition the mind and remain cool...under ALL conditions."(2)   ~unknown

Date ___/___/20__

STRESSFUL MOMENTS:

_____

_____

_____

HAPPY MOMENTS:

_____

_____

_____

PLAN AHEAD TODAY TO MINIMIZE YOUR STRESS TOMORROW.
(OR YOU CAN JUST WRITE OR DRAW SOMETHING SILLY DOWN BELOW AND GO TO
BED SMILING.)
PLANS FOR TOMORROW/TO DO LIST:

CREATE YOUR **OWN** INSPIRING **QUOTE** AND **SHARE YOUR WISDOM** WITH OTHERS!

_____

_____

Date ___/___/20__

STRESSFUL MOMENTS:

_____

_____

HAPPY MOMENTS:

_____

_____

Family Bonding Time...

-WRITE OR DRAW SOMETHING SILLY IN THE SPACE DOWN BELOW THAT WILL PUT A HUGE SMILE ON YOUR FACE. ALWAYS TRY TO GO TO BED SMILING AND FEELING HAPPY!

-THINK OF WAYS YOU CAN MAKE YOUR DAY EVEN BETTER TOMORROW.

-ALWAYS SHARE YOUR THOUGHTS AND CONCERNS (even when it is hard to do sometimes) WITH YOUR LOVING FAMILY FOR PROPER GUIDANCE AND GREAT IDEAS.

WRITE THEM DOWN BELOW IF NEEDED.

"Live life to express, not impress."(2)

Date ___/___/20__

STRESSFUL MOMENTS:

_____

_____

_____

HAPPY MOMENTS:

_____

_____

_____

PLAN AHEAD TODAY TO MINIMIZE YOUR STRESS TOMORROW.
(OR YOU CAN JUST WRITE OR DRAW SOMETHING SILLY DOWN BELOW AND GO TO
BED SMILING.)
PLANS FOR TOMORROW/TO DO LIST:

TIME FOR LAUGHS!

"Leave footprints of kindness wherever you go."(2)   ~unknown

Date ___/___/20__

STRESSFUL MOMENTS:

_____

_____

_____

HAPPY MOMENTS:

_____

_____

_____

PLAN AHEAD TODAY TO MINIMIZE YOUR STRESS TOMORROW.
(OR YOU CAN JUST WRITE OR DRAW SOMETHING SILLY DOWN BELOW AND GO TO
BED SMILING.)
PLANS FOR TOMORROW/TO DO LIST:

CREATE YOUR OWN INSPIRING QUOTE AND SHARE YOUR WISDOM WITH OTHERS!

_____

_____

Date ___/___/20__

STRESSFUL MOMENTS:

_____

_____

HAPPY MOMENTS:

_____

_____

Family Bonding Time...

-WRITE OR DRAW SOMETHING SILLY IN THE SPACE DOWN BELOW THAT WILL PUT A HUGE SMILE ON YOUR FACE. ALWAYS TRY TO GO TO BED SMILING AND FEELING HAPPY!

-THINK OF WAYS YOU CAN MAKE YOUR DAY EVEN BETTER TOMORROW.

-ALWAYS SHARE YOUR THOUGHTS AND CONCERNS (even when it is hard to do sometimes) WITH YOUR LOVING FAMILY FOR PROPER GUIDANCE AND GREAT IDEAS. WRITE THEM DOWN BELOW IF NEEDED.

"Collect moments...not things."(2) ~unknown

Date ___/___/20__

STRESSFUL MOMENTS:

_____

_____

_____

HAPPY MOMENTS:

_____

_____

_____

PLAN AHEAD TODAY TO MINIMIZE YOUR STRESS TOMORROW.
(OR YOU CAN JUST WRITE OR DRAW SOMETHING SILLY DOWN BELOW AND GO TO
BED SMILING.)
PLANS FOR TOMORROW/TO DO LIST:

CREATE YOUR OWN INSPIRING QUOTE AND SHARE YOUR WISDOM WITH OTHERS!

_____

_____

Date ___/___/20___

STRESSFUL MOMENTS:

_____

_____

HAPPY MOMENTS:

_____

_____

_____

Family Bonding Time...

-WRITE OR DRAW SOMETHING SILLY IN THE SPACE DOWN BELOW THAT WILL PUT A HUGE SMILE ON YOUR FACE. ALWAYS TRY TO GO TO BED SMILING AND FEELING HAPPY!

-THINK OF WAYS YOU CAN MAKE YOUR DAY EVEN BETTER TOMORROW.

-ALWAYS SHARE YOUR THOUGHTS AND CONCERNS (even when it is hard to do sometimes) WITH YOUR LOVING FAMILY FOR PROPER GUIDANCE AND GREAT IDEAS.

WRITE THEM DOWN BELOW IF NEEDED.

"True friendship isn't about being inseparable, it's being separated, and nothing changes."(2)

~unknown

Date ___/___/20__

STRESSFUL MOMENTS:

_____

_____

_____

HAPPY MOMENTS:

_____

_____

_____

PLAN AHEAD TODAY TO MINIMIZE YOUR STRESS TOMORROW.
(OR YOU CAN JUST WRITE OR DRAW SOMETHING SILLY DOWN BELOW AND GO TO BED SMILING.)
PLANS FOR TOMORROW/TO DO LIST:

CREATE YOUR **OWN** INSPIRING **QUOTE** AND **SHARE YOUR WISDOM** WITH OTHERS!

_____

_____

Date ___/___/20__

STRESSFUL MOMENTS:

_____

_____

HAPPY MOMENTS:

_____

_____

_____

Family Bonding Time...

-WRITE OR DRAW SOMETHING SILLY IN THE SPACE DOWN BELOW THAT WILL PUT A HUGE SMILE ON YOUR FACE. ALWAYS TRY TO GO TO BED SMILING AND FEELING HAPPY!

-THINK OF WAYS YOU CAN MAKE YOUR DAY EVEN BETTER TOMORROW.

-ALWAYS SHARE YOUR THOUGHTS AND CONCERNS (even when it is hard to do sometimes) WITH YOUR LOVING FAMILY FOR PROPER GUIDANCE AND GREAT IDEAS. WRITE THEM DOWN BELOW IF NEEDED.

"The shortest distance between new friends is...a smile."(2)   ~unknown

Date ___/___/20__

STRESSFUL MOMENTS:

_____

_____

_____

HAPPY MOMENTS:

_____

_____

_____

PLAN AHEAD TODAY TO MINIMIZE YOUR STRESS TOMORROW.
(OR YOU CAN JUST WRITE OR DRAW SOMETHING SILLY DOWN BELOW AND GO TO
BED SMILING.)
PLANS FOR TOMORROW/TO DO LIST:

CREATE YOUR **OWN** INSPIRING **QUOTE** AND **SHARE YOUR WISDOM**
WITH OTHERS!

_____

_____

Date ____/____/20___

STRESSFUL MOMENTS:

_____

_____

HAPPY MOMENTS:

_____

_____

Family Bonding Time...

-WRITE OR DRAW SOMETHING SILLY IN THE SPACE DOWN BELOW THAT WILL PUT A HUGE SMILE ON YOUR FACE. ALWAYS TRY TO GO TO BED SMILING AND FEELING HAPPY!

-THINK OF WAYS YOU CAN MAKE YOUR DAY EVEN BETTER TOMORROW.

-ALWAYS SHARE YOUR THOUGHTS AND CONCERNS (even when it is hard to do sometimes) WITH YOUR LOVING FAMILY FOR PROPER GUIDANCE AND GREAT IDEAS.

WRITE THEM DOWN BELOW IF NEEDED.

"As we grow up we realize it is less important to have lots of friends and more important to have REAL ones."(2)

~unknown

Date ___/___/20__

STRESSFUL MOMENTS:

_____

_____

_____

HAPPY MOMENTS:

_____

_____

_____

PLAN AHEAD TODAY TO MINIMIZE YOUR STRESS TOMORROW.
(OR YOU CAN JUST WRITE OR DRAW SOMETHING SILLY DOWN BELOW AND GO TO BED SMILING.)
PLANS FOR TOMORROW/TO DO LIST:

CREATE YOUR OWN INSPIRING QUOTE AND SHARE YOUR WISDOM WITH OTHERS!

_____

_____

Date ___/___/20__

STRESSFUL MOMENTS:

_____

_____

HAPPY MOMENTS:

_____

_____

_____

Family Bonding Time...

-WRITE OR DRAW SOMETHING SILLY IN THE SPACE DOWN BELOW THAT WILL PUT A HUGE SMILE ON YOUR FACE. ALWAYS TRY TO GO TO BED SMILING AND FEELING HAPPY!

-THINK OF WAYS YOU CAN MAKE YOUR DAY EVEN BETTER TOMORROW.

-ALWAYS SHARE YOUR THOUGHTS AND CONCERNS (even when it is hard to do sometimes) WITH YOUR LOVING FAMILY FOR PROPER GUIDANCE AND GREAT IDEAS.

WRITE THEM DOWN BELOW IF NEEDED.

A friend is someone who can make you smile no matter what!

Date ___/___/20__

STRESSFUL MOMENTS:

_____

_____

_____

HAPPY MOMENTS:

_____

_____

_____

PLAN AHEAD TODAY TO MINIMIZE YOUR STRESS TOMORROW.
(OR YOU CAN JUST WRITE OR DRAW SOMETHING SILLY DOWN BELOW AND GO TO BED SMILING.)
PLANS FOR TOMORROW/TO DO LIST:

CREATE YOUR OWN INSPIRING QUOTE AND SHARE YOUR WISDOM WITH OTHERS!

_____

_____

Date ___/___/20__

STRESSFUL MOMENTS:

_____

_____

HAPPY MOMENTS:

_____

_____

Family Bonding Time...

-WRITE OR DRAW SOMETHING SILLY IN THE SPACE DOWN BELOW THAT WILL PUT A HUGE SMILE ON YOUR FACE. ALWAYS TRY TO GO TO BED SMILING AND FEELING HAPPY!
-THINK OF WAYS YOU CAN MAKE YOUR DAY EVEN BETTER TOMORROW.
-ALWAYS SHARE YOUR THOUGHTS AND CONCERNS (even when it is hard to do sometimes) WITH YOUR LOVING FAMILY FOR PROPER GUIDANCE AND GREAT IDEAS. WRITE THEM DOWN BELOW IF NEEDED.

"When you look at a field of dandelions...you can either see a hundred weeds or a hundred wishes."(2)

~unknown

Date ___/___/20__

STRESSFUL MOMENTS:

_____

_____

_____

HAPPY MOMENTS:

_____

_____

_____

PLAN AHEAD TODAY TO MINIMIZE YOUR STRESS TOMORROW.
(OR YOU CAN JUST WRITE OR DRAW SOMETHING SILLY DOWN BELOW AND GO TO BED SMILING.)
PLANS FOR TOMORROW/TO DO LIST:

CREATE YOUR OWN INSPIRING QUOTE AND SHARE YOUR WISDOM WITH OTHERS!

_____

_____

Date ___/___/20__

STRESSFUL MOMENTS:

_____

_____

HAPPY MOMENTS:

_____

_____

Family Bonding Time...

-WRITE OR DRAW SOMETHING SILLY IN THE SPACE DOWN BELOW THAT WILL PUT A HUGE SMILE ON YOUR FACE. ALWAYS TRY TO GO TO BED SMILING AND FEELING HAPPY!

-THINK OF WAYS YOU CAN MAKE YOUR DAY EVEN BETTER TOMORROW.

-ALWAYS SHARE YOUR THOUGHTS AND CONCERNS (even when it is hard to do sometimes) WITH YOUR LOVING FAMILY FOR PROPER GUIDANCE AND GREAT IDEAS.

WRITE THEM DOWN BELOW IF NEEDED.

"There are always ten better things to do than just to give up."(2)   ~unknown

Date ___/___/20__

STRESSFUL MOMENTS:

_____

_____

_____

HAPPY MOMENTS:

_____

_____

_____

PLAN AHEAD TODAY TO MINIMIZE YOUR STRESS TOMORROW.
(OR YOU CAN JUST WRITE OR DRAW SOMETHING SILLY DOWN BELOW AND GO TO BED SMILING.)
PLANS FOR TOMORROW/TO DO LIST:

YOU ARE SOOOO LOVED!

"It doesn't matter if the glass is half full or half empty. Be grateful that you have a glass and there is something in it."(2)   ~unknown

Date ___/___/20__

STRESSFUL MOMENTS:

_____

_____

_____

HAPPY MOMENTS:

_____

_____

_____

PLAN AHEAD TODAY TO MINIMIZE YOUR STRESS TOMORROW.
(OR YOU CAN JUST WRITE OR DRAW SOMETHING SILLY DOWN BELOW AND GO TO BED SMILING.)
PLANS FOR TOMORROW/TO DO LIST:

CREATE YOUR OWN INSPIRING QUOTE AND SHARE YOUR WISDOM WITH OTHERS!

_____

_____

Date ___/___/20__

STRESSFUL MOMENTS:

_____

_____

HAPPY MOMENTS:

_____

_____

_____

Family Bonding Time...

-WRITE OR DRAW SOMETHING SILLY IN THE SPACE DOWN BELOW THAT WILL PUT A HUGE SMILE ON YOUR FACE. ALWAYS TRY TO GO TO BED FEELING HAPPY!. -THINK OF WAYS YOU CAN MAKE YOUR DAY EVEN BETTER TOMORROW. -ALWAYS SHARE YOUR THOUGHTS AND CONCERNS (even when it is hard to do sometimes) WITH YOUR LOVING FAMILY FOR PROPER GUIDANCE AND GREAT IDEAS.

WRITE THEM DOWN BELOW IF NEEDED.

"Inner peace begins the moment you choose not to allow another person or event to control your emotions."(2)

~unknown

Date ___/___/20__

STRESSFUL MOMENTS:

_____

_____

_____

HAPPY MOMENTS:

_____

_____

_____

PLAN AHEAD TODAY TO MINIMIZE YOUR STRESS TOMORROW.
(OR YOU CAN JUST WRITE OR DRAW SOMETHING SILLY DOWN BELOW AND GO TO BED SMILING.)
PLANS FOR TOMORROW/TO DO LIST:

245

CREATE YOUR **OWN** INSPIRING **QUOTE** AND **SHARE YOUR WISDOM** WITH OTHERS!

_____

_____

Date ___/___/20__

STRESSFUL MOMENTS:

_____

_____

HAPPY MOMENTS:

_____

_____

_____

Family Bonding Time...

-**WRITE OR DRAW SOMETHING SILLY IN THE SPACE DOWN BELOW THAT** WILL PUT A HUGE SMILE ON YOUR FACE. ALWAYS TRY TO GO TO BED FEELING HAPPY!
-**THINK** OF WAYS YOU CAN MAKE YOUR DAY EVEN BETTER TOMORROW.
-**ALWAYS SHARE** YOUR THOUGHTS AND CONCERNS (even when it is hard to do sometimes) WITH YOUR LOVING FAMILY FOR PROPER GUIDANCE AND GREAT IDEAS.

WRITE THEM DOWN BELOW IF NEEDED.

"If you don't believe in miracles, perhaps you've forgotten...You Are One."(2)

~unknown

Date ___/___/20__

STRESSFUL MOMENTS:

_____

_____

_____

HAPPY MOMENTS:

_____

_____

_____

PLAN AHEAD TODAY TO MINIMIZE YOUR STRESS TOMORROW.
(OR YOU CAN JUST WRITE OR DRAW SOMETHING SILLY DOWN BELOW AND GO TO BED SMILING.)
PLANS FOR TOMORROW/TO DO LIST:

CREATE YOUR OWN INSPIRING QUOTE AND SHARE YOUR WISDOM WITH OTHERS!

_____

_____

Date ___/___/20__

STRESSFUL MOMENTS:

_____

_____

HAPPY MOMENTS:

_____

_____

_____

Family Bonding Time...

-WRITE OR DRAW SOMETHING SILLY IN THE SPACE DOWN BELOW THAT WILL PUT A HUGE SMILE ON YOUR FACE. ALWAYS TRY TO GO TO BED FEELING HAPPY!
-THINK OF WAYS YOU CAN MAKE YOUR DAY EVEN BETTER TOMORROW.
-ALWAYS SHARE YOUR THOUGHTS AND CONCERNS (even when it is hard to do sometimes) WITH YOUR LOVING FAMILY FOR PROPER GUIDANCE AND GREAT IDEAS.

WRITE THEM DOWN BELOW IF NEEDED.

*"I am thankful for all those difficult people in my life. They have shown me who **I do not** want to be."*(2)

~unknown

Date ___/___/20__

STRESSFUL MOMENTS:

_____

_____

_____

HAPPY MOMENTS:

_____

_____

_____

PLAN AHEAD TODAY TO MINIMIZE YOUR STRESS TOMORROW.
(OR YOU CAN JUST WRITE OR DRAW SOMETHING SILLY DOWN BELOW AND GO TO BED SMILING.)
PLANS FOR TOMORROW/TO DO LIST:

CREATE YOUR OWN INSPIRING QUOTE AND SHARE YOUR WISDOM WITH OTHERS!

_____

_____

Date ___/___/20___

STRESSFUL MOMENTS:

_____

_____

HAPPY MOMENTS:

_____

_____

Family Bonding Time...

-WRITE OR DRAW SOMETHING SILLY IN THE SPACE DOWN BELOW THAT WILL PUT A HUGE SMILE ON YOUR FACE. ALWAYS TRY TO GO TO BED FEELING HAPPY!
-THINK OF WAYS YOU CAN MAKE YOUR DAY EVEN BETTER TOMORROW.
-ALWAYS SHARE YOUR THOUGHTS AND CONCERNS (even when it is hard to do sometimes) WITH YOUR LOVING FAMILY FOR PROPER GUIDANCE AND GREAT IDEAS.

WRITE THEM DOWN BELOW IF NEEDED.

"Forget all the reasons it won't work, and believe the one reason that it will."(2)

~unknown

Date ___/___/20__

STRESSFUL MOMENTS:

_____

_____

_____

HAPPY MOMENTS:

_____

_____

_____

PLAN AHEAD TODAY TO MINIMIZE YOUR STRESS TOMORROW.
(OR YOU CAN JUST WRITE OR DRAW SOMETHING SILLY DOWN BELOW AND GO TO BED SMILING.)
PLANS FOR TOMORROW/TO DO LIST:

CREATE YOUR **OWN** INSPIRING **QUOTE** AND **SHARE YOUR WISDOM** WITH OTHERS!

_____

_____

Date ___/___/20__

STRESSFUL MOMENTS:

_____

_____

HAPPY MOMENTS:

_____

_____

Family Bonding Time...

-WRITE OR DRAW SOMETHING SILLY IN THE SPACE DOWN BELOW THAT WILL PUT A HUGE SMILE ON YOUR FACE. ALWAYS TRY TO GO TO BED FEELING HAPPY! **-THINK** OF WAYS YOU CAN MAKE YOUR DAY EVEN BETTER TOMORROW. **-ALWAYS SHARE** YOUR THOUGHTS AND CONCERNS (even when it is hard to do sometimes) WITH YOUR LOVING FAMILY FOR PROPER GUIDANCE AND GREAT IDEAS. WRITE THEM DOWN BELOW IF NEEDED.

"Every positive thought propels you in the right direction."(2)   ~unknown

Date ___/___/20__

STRESSFUL MOMENTS:

_____

_____

_____

HAPPY MOMENTS:

_____

_____

_____

PLAN AHEAD TODAY TO MINIMIZE YOUR STRESS TOMORROW.
(OR YOU CAN JUST WRITE OR DRAW SOMETHING SILLY DOWN BELOW AND GO TO
BED SMILING.)
PLANS FOR TOMORROW/TO DO LIST:

CREATE YOUR OWN INSPIRING QUOTE AND SHARE YOUR WISDOM WITH OTHERS!

_____

_____

Date ___/___/20__

STRESSFUL MOMENTS:

_____

_____

HAPPY MOMENTS:

_____

_____

_____

Family Bonding Time...

-WRITE OR DRAW SOMETHING SILLY IN THE SPACE DOWN BELOW THAT WILL PUT A HUGE SMILE ON YOUR FACE. ALWAYS TRY TO GO TO BED FEELING HAPPY!
-THINK OF WAYS YOU CAN MAKE YOUR DAY EVEN BETTER TOMORROW.
-ALWAYS SHARE YOUR THOUGHTS AND CONCERNS (even when it is hard to do sometimes) WITH YOUR LOVING FAMILY FOR PROPER GUIDANCE AND GREAT IDEAS.
WRITE THEM DOWN BELOW IF NEEDED.

"Believe it...in your mind. Receive it...in your heart. Achieve it...in your life."(2)

~unknown

Date ___/___/20__

STRESSFUL MOMENTS:

_____

_____

_____

HAPPY MOMENTS:

_____

_____

_____

PLAN AHEAD TODAY TO MINIMIZE YOUR STRESS TOMORROW.
(OR YOU CAN JUST WRITE OR DRAW SOMETHING SILLY DOWN BELOW AND GO TO BED SMILING.)
PLANS FOR TOMORROW/TO DO LIST:

ENJOY EVERY MOMENT

Date ___/___/20__

STRESSFUL MOMENTS:

_____

_____

_____

HAPPY MOMENTS:

_____

_____

_____

PLAN AHEAD TODAY TO MINIMIZE YOUR STRESS TOMORROW.
(OR YOU CAN JUST WRITE OR DRAW SOMETHING SILLY DOWN BELOW AND GO TO BED SMILING.)
PLANS FOR TOMORROW/TO DO LIST:

CREATE YOUR OWN INSPIRING QUOTE AND SHARE YOUR WISDOM WITH OTHERS!

_____

_____

Date ___/___/20___

STRESSFUL MOMENTS:

_____

_____

HAPPY MOMENTS:

_____

_____

_____

Family Bonding Time...

-WRITE OR DRAW SOMETHING SILLY IN THE SPACE DOWN BELOW THAT WILL PUT A HUGE SMILE ON YOUR FACE. ALWAYS TRY TO GO TO BED SMILING AND FEELING HAPPY!

-THINK OF WAYS YOU CAN MAKE YOUR DAY EVEN BETTER TOMORROW.

-ALWAYS SHARE YOUR THOUGHTS AND CONCERNS (even when it is hard to do sometimes) WITH YOUR LOVING FAMILY FOR PROPER GUIDANCE AND GREAT IDEAS. WRITE THEM DOWN BELOW IF NEEDED.

"Always remember that your present situation is not your final destination. The best is yet to come."(2)

Date ___/___/20__

STRESSFUL MOMENTS:

_____

_____

_____

HAPPY MOMENTS:

_____

_____

_____

PLAN AHEAD TODAY TO MINIMIZE YOUR STRESS TOMORROW.
(OR YOU CAN JUST WRITE OR DRAW SOMETHING SILLY DOWN BELOW AND GO TO BED SMILING.)
PLANS FOR TOMORROW/TO DO LIST:

CREATE YOUR **OWN** INSPIRING **QUOTE** AND **SHARE YOUR WISDOM** WITH OTHERS!

_____

_____

Date ___/___/20__

STRESSFUL MOMENTS:

_____

_____

HAPPY MOMENTS:

_____

_____

Family Bonding Time...

-WRITE OR DRAW SOMETHING SILLY IN THE SPACE DOWN BELOW THAT WILL PUT A HUGE SMILE ON YOUR FACE. ALWAYS TRY TO GO TO BED SMILING AND FEELING HAPPY!

-THINK OF WAYS YOU CAN MAKE YOUR DAY EVEN BETTER TOMORROW.

-ALWAYS SHARE YOUR THOUGHTS AND CONCERNS (even when it is hard to do sometimes) WITH YOUR LOVING FAMILY FOR PROPER GUIDANCE AND GREAT IDEAS.

WRITE THEM DOWN BELOW IF NEEDED.

"A good life is when you smile often, dream big, laugh a lot, and realize how blessed you are for what you have."(2)

~unknown

Date ___/___/20__

STRESSFUL MOMENTS:

_____

_____

_____

HAPPY MOMENTS:

_____

_____

_____

PLAN AHEAD TODAY TO MINIMIZE YOUR STRESS TOMORROW.
(OR YOU CAN JUST WRITE OR DRAW SOMETHING SILLY DOWN BELOW AND GO TO BED SMILING.)
PLANS FOR TOMORROW/TO DO LIST:

CREATE YOUR OWN INSPIRING QUOTE AND SHARE YOUR WISDOM WITH OTHERS!

_____

_____

Date ___/___/20___

STRESSFUL MOMENTS:

_____

_____

HAPPY MOMENTS:

_____

_____

_____

Family Bonding Time...

-WRITE OR DRAW SOMETHING SILLY IN THE SPACE DOWN BELOW THAT WILL PUT A HUGE SMILE ON YOUR FACE. ALWAYS TRY TO GO TO BED SMILING AND FEELING HAPPY!

-THINK OF WAYS YOU CAN MAKE YOUR DAY EVEN BETTER TOMORROW.

-ALWAYS SHARE YOUR THOUGHTS AND CONCERNS (even when it is hard to do sometimes) WITH YOUR LOVING FAMILY FOR PROPER GUIDANCE AND GREAT IDEAS. WRITE THEM DOWN BELOW IF NEEDED.

Make sure that you always remember - you are one of a kind, and you have something great to offer to others!

Date ___/___/20__

STRESSFUL MOMENTS:

_____

_____

_____

HAPPY MOMENTS:

_____

_____

_____

PLAN AHEAD TODAY TO MINIMIZE YOUR STRESS TOMORROW.
(OR YOU CAN JUST WRITE OR DRAW SOMETHING SILLY DOWN BELOW AND GO TO BED SMILING.)
PLANS FOR TOMORROW/TO DO LIST:

CREATE YOUR OWN INSPIRING QUOTE AND SHARE YOUR WISDOM WITH OTHERS!

_____

_____

Date ___/___/20__

STRESSFUL MOMENTS:

_____

_____

HAPPY MOMENTS:

_____

_____

Family Bonding Time...

-WRITE OR DRAW SOMETHING SILLY IN THE SPACE DOWN BELOW THAT WILL PUT A HUGE SMILE ON YOUR FACE. ALWAYS TRY TO GO TO BED SMILING AND FEELING HAPPY!

-THINK OF WAYS YOU CAN MAKE YOUR DAY EVEN BETTER TOMORROW.

-ALWAYS SHARE YOUR THOUGHTS AND CONCERNS (even when it is hard to do sometimes) WITH YOUR LOVING FAMILY FOR PROPER GUIDANCE AND GREAT IDEAS.

WRITE THEM DOWN BELOW IF NEEDED.

"Never look back unless you are planning to go that way."[1]
~Henry David Thoreau

Date ___/___/20__

STRESSFUL MOMENTS:

_____

_____

_____

HAPPY MOMENTS:

_____

_____

_____

PLAN AHEAD TODAY TO MINIMIZE YOUR STRESS TOMORROW.
(OR YOU CAN JUST WRITE OR DRAW SOMETHING SILLY DOWN BELOW AND GO TO BED SMILING.)
PLANS FOR TOMORROW/TO DO LIST:

CREATE YOUR OWN INSPIRING QUOTE AND SHARE YOUR WISDOM WITH OTHERS!

_____

_____

Date ___/___/20__

STRESSFUL MOMENTS:

_____

_____

HAPPY MOMENTS:

_____

_____

Family Bonding Time...

-WRITE OR DRAW SOMETHING SILLY IN THE SPACE DOWN BELOW THAT WILL PUT A HUGE SMILE ON YOUR FACE. ALWAYS TRY TO GO TO BED SMILING AND FEELING HAPPY!

-THINK OF WAYS YOU CAN MAKE YOUR DAY EVEN BETTER TOMORROW.

-ALWAYS SHARE YOUR THOUGHTS AND CONCERNS (even when it is hard to do sometimes) WITH YOUR LOVING FAMILY FOR PROPER GUIDANCE AND GREAT IDEAS.

WRITE THEM DOWN BELOW IF NEEDED.

"What is once well done is done forever."[1]   ~Henry David Thoreau

Date ___/___/20__

STRESSFUL MOMENTS:

_____

_____

_____

HAPPY MOMENTS:

_____

_____

_____

PLAN AHEAD TODAY TO MINIMIZE YOUR STRESS TOMORROW.
(OR YOU CAN JUST WRITE OR DRAW SOMETHING SILLY DOWN BELOW AND GO TO BED SMILING.)
PLANS FOR TOMORROW/TO DO LIST:

CREATE YOUR OWN INSPIRING QUOTE AND SHARE YOUR WISDOM WITH OTHERS!

_____

_____

Date ___/___/20__

STRESSFUL MOMENTS:

_____

_____

HAPPY MOMENTS:

_____

_____

Family Bonding Time...

-WRITE OR DRAW SOMETHING SILLY IN THE SPACE DOWN BELOW THAT WILL PUT A HUGE SMILE ON YOUR FACE. ALWAYS TRY TO GO TO BED SMILING AND FEELING HAPPY!

-THINK OF WAYS YOU CAN MAKE YOUR DAY EVEN BETTER TOMORROW.

-ALWAYS SHARE YOUR THOUGHTS AND CONCERNS (even when it is hard to do sometimes) WITH YOUR LOVING FAMILY FOR PROPER GUIDANCE AND GREAT IDEAS.

WRITE THEM DOWN BELOW IF NEEDED.

"Go confidently in the direction of your dreams. Live the life you have imagined."(2)

~H.D. Thoreau

Date ___/___/20__

STRESSFUL MOMENTS:

_____

_____

_____

HAPPY MOMENTS:

_____

_____

_____

PLAN AHEAD TODAY TO MINIMIZE YOUR STRESS TOMORROW.
(OR YOU CAN JUST WRITE OR DRAW SOMETHING SILLY DOWN BELOW AND GO TO BED SMILING.)
PLANS FOR TOMORROW/TO DO LIST:

CREATE YOUR OWN INSPIRING QUOTE AND SHARE YOUR WISDOM WITH OTHERS!

_____

_____

Date ___/___/20__

STRESSFUL MOMENTS:

_____

_____

HAPPY MOMENTS:

_____

_____

Family Bonding Time...

-WRITE OR DRAW SOMETHING SILLY IN THE SPACE DOWN BELOW THAT WILL PUT A HUGE SMILE ON YOUR FACE. ALWAYS TRY TO GO TO BED SMILING AND FEELING HAPPY!

-THINK OF WAYS YOU CAN MAKE YOUR DAY EVEN BETTER TOMORROW.

-ALWAYS SHARE YOUR THOUGHTS AND CONCERNS (even when it is hard to do sometimes) WITH YOUR LOVING FAMILY FOR PROPER GUIDANCE AND GREAT IDEAS.

WRITE THEM DOWN BELOW IF NEEDED.

You have a fantastic ability to dream higher than the sky!

Date ___/___/20__

STRESSFUL MOMENTS:

_____

_____

_____

HAPPY MOMENTS:

_____

_____

_____

PLAN AHEAD TODAY TO MINIMIZE YOUR STRESS TOMORROW.
(OR YOU CAN JUST WRITE OR DRAW SOMETHING SILLY DOWN BELOW AND GO TO BED SMILING.)
PLANS FOR TOMORROW/TO DO LIST:

TIME FOR HUGS!

"Believe in yourself and you can do unbelievable things."(2)   ~unknown

Date ___/___/20__

STRESSFUL MOMENTS:

_____

_____

_____

HAPPY MOMENTS:

_____

_____

_____

PLAN AHEAD TODAY TO MINIMIZE YOUR STRESS TOMORROW.
(OR YOU CAN JUST WRITE OR DRAW SOMETHING SILLY DOWN BELOW AND GO TO BED SMILING.)
PLANS FOR TOMORROW/TO DO LIST:

CREATE YOUR **OWN** INSPIRING **QUOTE** AND **SHARE YOUR WISDOM**
WITH OTHERS!

_____

_____

Date ___/___/20___

STRESSFUL MOMENTS:

_____

_____

HAPPY MOMENTS:

_____

_____

_____

Family Bonding Time...

-WRITE OR DRAW SOMETHING SILLY IN THE SPACE DOWN BELOW THAT WILL PUT A HUGE SMILE ON YOUR FACE. ALWAYS TRY TO GO TO BED SMILING AND FEELING HAPPY!
-THINK OF WAYS YOU CAN MAKE YOUR DAY EVEN BETTER TOMORROW.
-ALWAYS SHARE YOUR THOUGHTS AND CONCERNS (even when it is hard to do sometimes) WITH YOUR LOVING FAMILY FOR PROPER GUIDANCE AND GREAT IDEAS.

WRITE THEM DOWN BELOW IF NEEDED.

"The most wasted of all days is one without laughter."(2)   ~unknown

Date ___/___/20__

STRESSFUL MOMENTS:

_____

_____

_____

HAPPY MOMENTS:

_____

_____

_____

PLAN AHEAD TODAY TO MINIMIZE YOUR STRESS TOMORROW.
(OR YOU CAN JUST WRITE OR DRAW SOMETHING SILLY DOWN BELOW AND GO TO
BED SMILING.)
PLANS FOR TOMORROW/TO DO LIST:

CREATE YOUR OWN INSPIRING QUOTE AND SHARE YOUR WISDOM WITH OTHERS!

_____

_____

Date ___/___/20__

STRESSFUL MOMENTS:

_____

_____

HAPPY MOMENTS:

_____

_____

Family Bonding Time...

-WRITE OR DRAW SOMETHING SILLY IN THE SPACE DOWN BELOW THAT WILL PUT A HUGE SMILE ON YOUR FACE. ALWAYS TRY TO GO TO BED SMILING AND FEELING HAPPY!

-THINK OF WAYS YOU CAN MAKE YOUR DAY EVEN BETTER TOMORROW.

-ALWAYS SHARE YOUR THOUGHTS AND CONCERNS (even when it is hard to do sometimes) WITH YOUR LOVING FAMILY FOR PROPER GUIDANCE AND GREAT IDEAS.

WRITE THEM DOWN BELOW IF NEEDED.

"We can't control what others say about us, but we can control what we choose to believe."(2)

~unknown

Date ___/___/20__

STRESSFUL MOMENTS:

_____

_____

_____

HAPPY MOMENTS:

_____

_____

_____

PLAN AHEAD TODAY TO MINIMIZE YOUR STRESS TOMORROW.
(OR YOU CAN JUST WRITE OR DRAW SOMETHING SILLY DOWN BELOW AND GO TO BED SMILING.)
PLANS FOR TOMORROW/TO DO LIST:

CREATE YOUR OWN INSPIRING QUOTE AND SHARE YOUR WISDOM WITH OTHERS!

_____

_____

Date ___/___/20__

STRESSFUL MOMENTS:

_____

_____

HAPPY MOMENTS:

_____

_____

_____

Family Bonding Time…

-WRITE OR DRAW SOMETHING SILLY IN THE SPACE DOWN BELOW THAT WILL PUT A HUGE SMILE ON YOUR FACE. ALWAYS TRY TO GO TO BED SMILING AND FEELING HAPPY!

-THINK OF WAYS YOU CAN MAKE YOUR DAY EVEN BETTER TOMORROW.

-ALWAYS SHARE YOUR THOUGHTS AND CONCERNS (even when it is hard to do sometimes) WITH YOUR LOVING FAMILY FOR PROPER GUIDANCE AND GREAT IDEAS.

WRITE THEM DOWN BELOW IF NEEDED.

If you spend all of your time with negative people - you will become like them. Try your best always to stay positive even if it feels like your life is falling apart!

Date ___/___/20__

STRESSFUL MOMENTS:

_____

_____

_____

HAPPY MOMENTS:

_____

_____

_____

PLAN AHEAD TODAY TO MINIMIZE YOUR STRESS TOMORROW.
(OR YOU CAN JUST WRITE OR DRAW SOMETHING SILLY DOWN BELOW AND GO TO BED SMILING.)
PLANS FOR TOMORROW/TO DO LIST:

CREATE YOUR OWN INSPIRING QUOTE AND SHARE YOUR WISDOM WITH OTHERS!

_____

_____

Date ___/___/20__

STRESSFUL MOMENTS:

_____

_____

HAPPY MOMENTS:

_____

_____

Family Bonding Time…

-WRITE OR DRAW SOMETHING SILLY IN THE SPACE DOWN BELOW THAT WILL PUT A HUGE SMILE ON YOUR FACE. ALWAYS TRY TO GO TO BED SMILING AND FEELING HAPPY!

-THINK OF WAYS YOU CAN MAKE YOUR DAY EVEN BETTER TOMORROW.

-ALWAYS SHARE YOUR THOUGHTS AND CONCERNS (even when it is hard to do sometimes) WITH YOUR LOVING FAMILY FOR PROPER GUIDANCE AND GREAT IDEAS. WRITE THEM DOWN BELOW IF NEEDED.

"To get something you've never had, you have to do something you've never done."(2)

~unknown

Date ___/___/20___

STRESSFUL MOMENTS:

_____

_____

_____

HAPPY MOMENTS:

_____

_____

_____

PLAN AHEAD TODAY TO MINIMIZE YOUR STRESS TOMORROW.
(OR YOU CAN JUST WRITE OR DRAW SOMETHING SILLY DOWN BELOW AND GO TO BED SMILING.)
PLANS FOR TOMORROW/TO DO LIST:

CREATE YOUR **OWN** INSPIRING **QUOTE** AND **SHARE YOUR WISDOM** WITH OTHERS!

_____

_____

Date ___/___/20___

STRESSFUL MOMENTS:

_____

_____

HAPPY MOMENTS:

_____

_____

Family Bonding Time...

-WRITE OR DRAW SOMETHING SILLY IN THE SPACE DOWN BELOW THAT WILL PUT A HUGE SMILE ON YOUR FACE. ALWAYS TRY TO GO TO BED SMILING AND FEELING HAPPY!

-THINK OF WAYS YOU CAN MAKE YOUR DAY EVEN BETTER TOMORROW.

-ALWAYS SHARE YOUR THOUGHTS AND CONCERNS (even when it is hard to do sometimes) WITH YOUR LOVING FAMILY FOR PROPER GUIDANCE AND GREAT IDEAS. WRITE THEM DOWN BELOW IF NEEDED.

Respect others as you want others to respect you.

Date ___/___/20__

STRESSFUL MOMENTS:

_____

_____

_____

HAPPY MOMENTS:

_____

_____

_____

PLAN AHEAD TODAY TO MINIMIZE YOUR STRESS TOMORROW.
(OR YOU CAN JUST WRITE OR DRAW SOMETHING SILLY DOWN BELOW AND GO TO BED SMILING.)
PLANS FOR TOMORROW/TO DO LIST:

CREATE YOUR OWN INSPIRING QUOTE AND SHARE YOUR WISDOM WITH OTHERS!

_____

_____

Date ___/___/20___

STRESSFUL MOMENTS:

_____

_____

HAPPY MOMENTS:

_____

_____

_____

Family Bonding Time...

-WRITE OR DRAW SOMETHING SILLY IN THE SPACE DOWN BELOW THAT WILL PUT A HUGE SMILE ON YOUR FACE. ALWAYS TRY TO GO TO BED SMILING AND FEELING HAPPY!

-THINK OF WAYS YOU CAN MAKE YOUR DAY EVEN BETTER TOMORROW.

-ALWAYS SHARE YOUR THOUGHTS AND CONCERNS (even when it is hard to do sometimes) WITH YOUR LOVING FAMILY FOR PROPER GUIDANCE AND GREAT IDEAS. WRITE THEM DOWN BELOW IF NEEDED.

A moment MAD is a moment of happiness LOST FOREVER!!!

Date ___/___/20__

STRESSFUL MOMENTS:

_____

_____

_____

HAPPY MOMENTS:

_____

_____

_____

PLAN AHEAD TODAY TO MINIMIZE YOUR STRESS TOMORROW.
(OR YOU CAN JUST WRITE OR DRAW SOMETHING SILLY DOWN BELOW AND GO TO BED SMILING.)
PLANS FOR TOMORROW/TO DO LIST:

CREATE YOUR OWN INSPIRING QUOTE AND SHARE YOUR WISDOM WITH OTHERS!

_____

_____

Date ___/___/20__

STRESSFUL MOMENTS:

_____

_____

HAPPY MOMENTS:

_____

_____

_____

Family Bonding Time…

-WRITE OR DRAW SOMETHING SILLY IN THE SPACE DOWN BELOW THAT WILL PUT A HUGE SMILE ON YOUR FACE. ALWAYS TRY TO GO TO BED SMILING AND FEELING HAPPY!

-THINK OF WAYS YOU CAN MAKE YOUR DAY EVEN BETTER TOMORROW.

-ALWAYS SHARE YOUR THOUGHTS AND CONCERNS (even when it is hard to do sometimes) WITH YOUR LOVING FAMILY FOR PROPER GUIDANCE AND GREAT IDEAS.

WRITE THEM DOWN BELOW IF NEEDED.

You are FREE to choose, but you will ALWAYS be responsible for your OWN choices!

Date ___/___/20__

STRESSFUL MOMENTS:

_____

_____

_____

HAPPY MOMENTS:

_____

_____

_____

PLAN AHEAD TODAY TO MINIMIZE YOUR STRESS TOMORROW.
(OR YOU CAN JUST WRITE OR DRAW SOMETHING SILLY DOWN BELOW AND GO TO BED SMILING.)
PLANS FOR TOMORROW/TO DO LIST:

CREATE YOUR OWN INSPIRING QUOTE AND SHARE YOUR WISDOM WITH OTHERS!

_____

_____

Date ___/___/20__

STRESSFUL MOMENTS:

_____

_____

HAPPY MOMENTS:

_____

_____

_____

Family Bonding Time...

-WRITE OR DRAW SOMETHING SILLY IN THE SPACE DOWN BELOW THAT WILL PUT A HUGE SMILE ON YOUR FACE. ALWAYS TRY TO GO TO BED SMILING AND FEELING HAPPY!

-THINK OF WAYS YOU CAN MAKE YOUR DAY EVEN BETTER TOMORROW.

-ALWAYS SHARE YOUR THOUGHTS AND CONCERNS (even when it is hard to do sometimes) WITH YOUR LOVING FAMILY FOR PROPER GUIDANCE AND GREAT IDEAS.

WRITE THEM DOWN BELOW IF NEEDED.

"STOP hating yourself for everything you aren't. START loving yourself for everything that you are."(2)

~unknown

Date ___ / ___ /20__

STRESSFUL MOMENTS:

_____

_____

_____

HAPPY MOMENTS:

_____

_____

_____

PLAN AHEAD TODAY TO MINIMIZE YOUR STRESS TOMORROW.
(OR YOU CAN JUST WRITE OR DRAW SOMETHING SILLY DOWN BELOW AND GO TO BED SMILING.)
PLANS FOR TOMORROW/TO DO LIST:

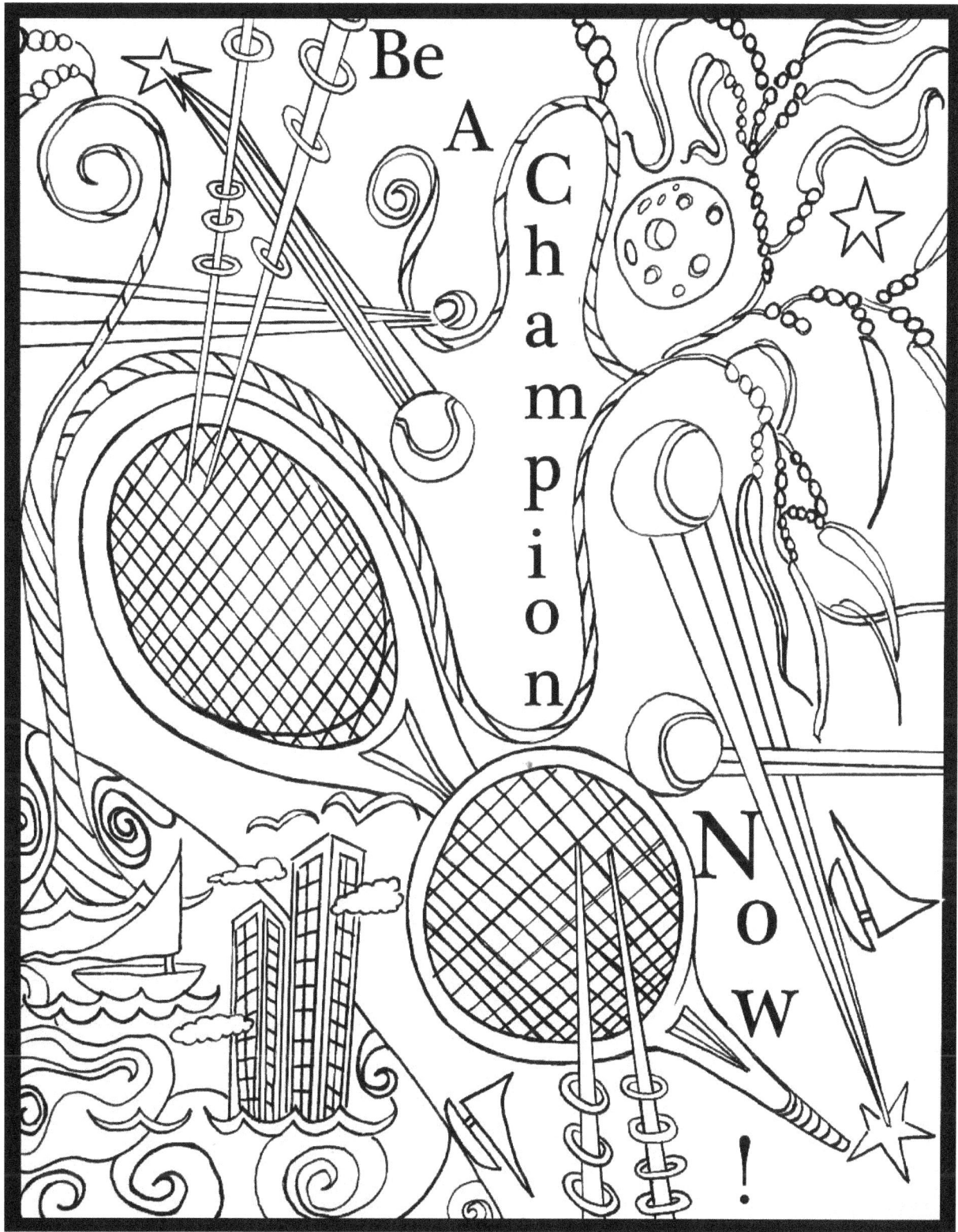

Be A Champion Now!

Remind yourself often - it is okay not to be perfect.

Date ___/___/20__

STRESSFUL MOMENTS:

_____

_____

_____

HAPPY MOMENTS:

_____

_____

_____

PLAN AHEAD TODAY TO MINIMIZE YOUR STRESS TOMORROW.
(OR YOU CAN JUST WRITE OR DRAW SOMETHING SILLY DOWN BELOW AND GO TO
BED SMILING.)
PLANS FOR TOMORROW/TO DO LIST:

CREATE YOUR OWN INSPIRING QUOTE AND SHARE YOUR WISDOM WITH OTHERS!

_____

_____

Date ___/___/20__

STRESSFUL MOMENTS:

_____

_____

HAPPY MOMENTS:

_____

_____

_____

Family Bonding Time...

-WRITE OR DRAW SOMETHING SILLY IN THE SPACE DOWN BELOW THAT WILL PUT A HUGE SMILE ON YOUR FACE. ALWAYS TRY TO GO TO BED SMILING AND FEELING HAPPY!

-THINK OF WAYS YOU CAN MAKE YOUR DAY EVEN BETTER TOMORROW.

-ALWAYS SHARE YOUR THOUGHTS AND CONCERNS (even when it is hard to do sometimes) WITH YOUR LOVING FAMILY FOR PROPER GUIDANCE AND GREAT IDEAS.

WRITE THEM DOWN BELOW IF NEEDED.

"Your thoughts create your future: DREAM, BELIEVE, ACHIEVE!!!"(2)
~unknown

Date ___/___/20__

STRESSFUL MOMENTS:

_____

_____

_____

HAPPY MOMENTS:

_____

_____

_____

PLAN AHEAD TODAY TO MINIMIZE YOUR STRESS TOMORROW.
(OR YOU CAN JUST WRITE OR DRAW SOMETHING SILLY DOWN BELOW AND GO TO BED SMILING.)
PLANS FOR TOMORROW/TO DO LIST:

CREATE YOUR **OWN** INSPIRING **QUOTE** AND **SHARE YOUR WISDOM WITH OTHERS!**

_____

_____

Date ___/___/20__

STRESSFUL MOMENTS:

_____

_____

HAPPY MOMENTS:

_____

_____

_____

Family Bonding Time…

-**WRITE OR DRAW SOMETHING SILLY IN THE SPACE DOWN BELOW THAT** WILL PUT A HUGE SMILE ON YOUR FACE. ALWAYS TRY TO GO TO BED SMILING AND FEELING HAPPY!

-**THINK** OF WAYS YOU CAN MAKE YOUR DAY EVEN BETTER TOMORROW.

-**ALWAYS SHARE** YOUR THOUGHTS AND CONCERNS (even when it is hard to do sometimes) WITH YOUR LOVING FAMILY FOR PROPER GUIDANCE AND GREAT IDEAS.

WRITE THEM DOWN BELOW IF NEEDED.

"Don't trust words - trust actions."(2)   ~unknown

Date ___/___/20__

STRESSFUL MOMENTS:

_____

_____

_____

HAPPY MOMENTS:

_____

_____

_____

PLAN AHEAD TODAY TO MINIMIZE YOUR STRESS TOMORROW.
(OR YOU CAN JUST WRITE OR DRAW SOMETHING SILLY DOWN BELOW AND GO TO BED SMILING.)
PLANS FOR TOMORROW/TO DO LIST:

CREATE YOUR **OWN** INSPIRING **QUOTE** AND **SHARE YOUR WISDOM** WITH OTHERS!

_____

_____

Date ___/___/20__

STRESSFUL MOMENTS:

_____

_____

HAPPY MOMENTS:

_____

_____

_____

Family Bonding Time...

-WRITE OR DRAW SOMETHING SILLY IN THE SPACE DOWN BELOW THAT WILL PUT A HUGE SMILE ON YOUR FACE. ALWAYS TRY TO GO TO BED SMILING AND FEELING HAPPY!

-THINK OF WAYS YOU CAN MAKE YOUR DAY EVEN BETTER TOMORROW.

-ALWAYS SHARE YOUR THOUGHTS AND CONCERNS (even when it is hard to do sometimes) WITH YOUR LOVING FAMILY FOR PROPER GUIDANCE AND GREAT IDEAS.

WRITE THEM DOWN BELOW IF NEEDED.

"Life is like an elevator. You will go through ups and downs. But only you will be in charge of which direction it goes."(2)

~unknown

Date ___/___/20__

STRESSFUL MOMENTS:

_____

_____

_____

HAPPY MOMENTS:

_____

_____

_____

PLAN AHEAD TODAY TO MINIMIZE YOUR STRESS TOMORROW.
(OR YOU CAN JUST WRITE OR DRAW SOMETHING SILLY DOWN BELOW AND GO TO BED SMILING.)
PLANS FOR TOMORROW/TO DO LIST:

297

CREATE YOUR OWN INSPIRING QUOTE AND SHARE YOUR WISDOM WITH OTHERS!

_____

_____

Date ___/___/20__

STRESSFUL MOMENTS:

_____

_____

HAPPY MOMENTS:

_____

_____

Family Bonding Time…

-WRITE OR DRAW SOMETHING SILLY IN THE SPACE DOWN BELOW THAT WILL PUT A HUGE SMILE ON YOUR FACE. ALWAYS TRY TO GO TO BED SMILING AND FEELING HAPPY!

-THINK OF WAYS YOU CAN MAKE YOUR DAY EVEN BETTER TOMORROW.

-ALWAYS SHARE YOUR THOUGHTS AND CONCERNS (even when it is hard to do sometimes) WITH YOUR LOVING FAMILY FOR PROPER GUIDANCE AND GREAT IDEAS.

WRITE THEM DOWN BELOW IF NEEDED.

"Your ATTITUDE is like a price tag; it shown how VALUABLE you are."(2)
~unknown

Date ___/___/20__

STRESSFUL MOMENTS:

_____

_____

_____

HAPPY MOMENTS:

_____

_____

_____

PLAN AHEAD TODAY TO MINIMIZE YOUR STRESS TOMORROW.
(OR YOU CAN JUST WRITE OR DRAW SOMETHING SILLY DOWN BELOW AND GO TO BED SMILING.)
PLANS FOR TOMORROW/TO DO LIST:

CREATE YOUR OWN INSPIRING QUOTE AND SHARE YOUR WISDOM WITH OTHERS!

_____

_____

Date ___/___/20__

STRESSFUL MOMENTS:

_____

_____

HAPPY MOMENTS:

_____

_____

Family Bonding Time...

-WRITE OR DRAW SOMETHING SILLY IN THE SPACE DOWN BELOW THAT WILL PUT A HUGE SMILE ON YOUR FACE. ALWAYS TRY TO GO TO BED SMILING AND FEELING HAPPY!

-THINK OF WAYS YOU CAN MAKE YOUR DAY EVEN BETTER TOMORROW.

-ALWAYS SHARE YOUR THOUGHTS AND CONCERNS (even when it is hard to do sometimes) WITH YOUR LOVING FAMILY FOR PROPER GUIDANCE AND GREAT IDEAS.

WRITE THEM DOWN BELOW IF NEEDED.

"The two most important days in your life are the day you were born and the day you will find out why."(2)
~Mark Twain

Date ___/___/20__

STRESSFUL MOMENTS:

_____

_____

_____

HAPPY MOMENTS:

_____

_____

_____

PLAN AHEAD TODAY TO MINIMIZE YOUR STRESS TOMORROW.
(OR YOU CAN JUST WRITE OR DRAW SOMETHING SILLY DOWN BELOW AND GO TO BED SMILING.)
PLANS FOR TOMORROW/TO DO LIST:

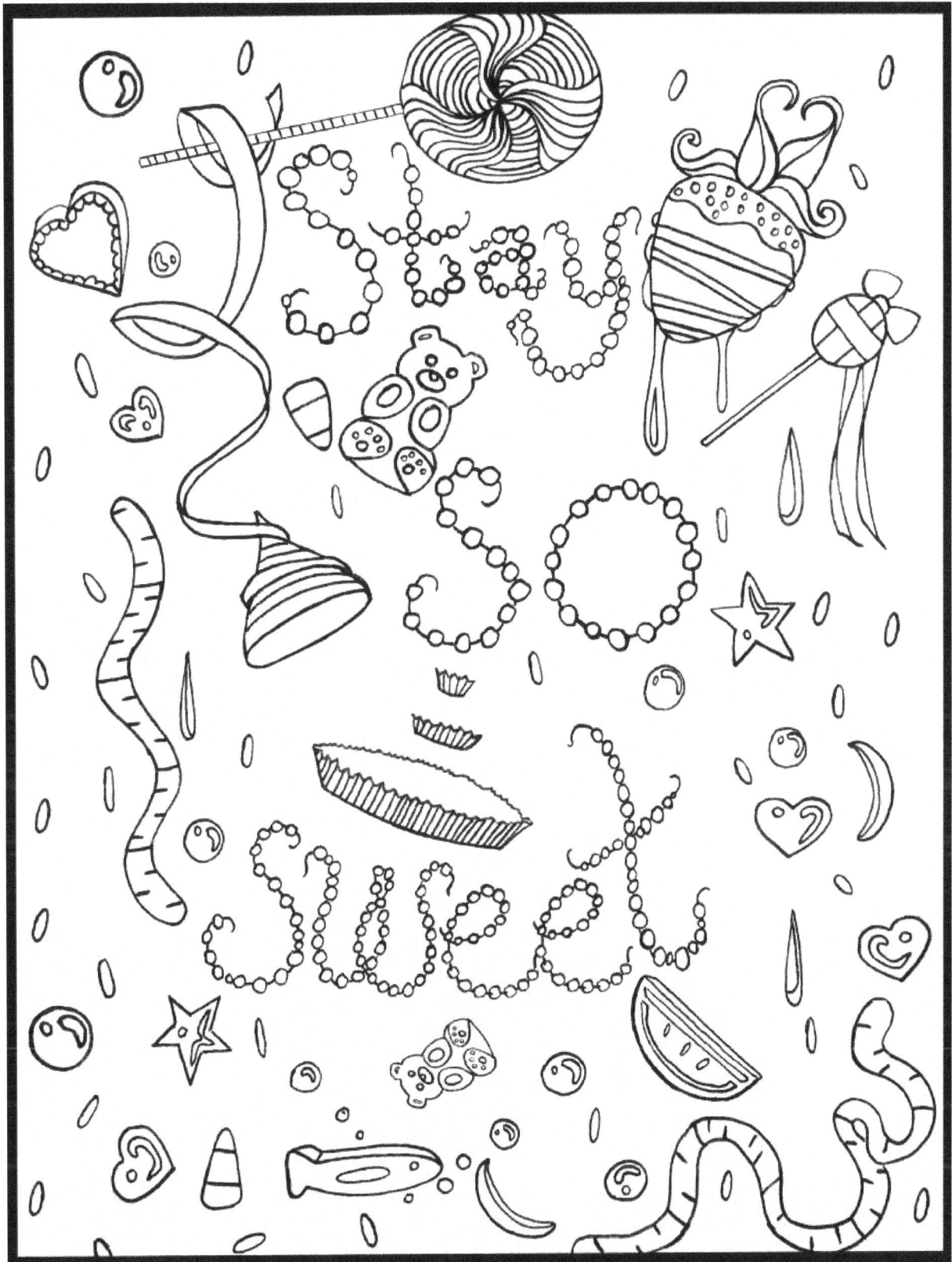

"Don't be ashamed of your story - IT WILL inspire others."(2)   ~unknown

Date ___/___/20__

STRESSFUL MOMENTS:

_____

_____

_____

HAPPY MOMENTS:

_____

_____

_____

PLAN AHEAD TODAY TO MINIMIZE YOUR STRESS TOMORROW.
(OR YOU CAN JUST WRITE OR DRAW SOMETHING SILLY DOWN BELOW AND GO TO BED SMILING.)
PLANS FOR TOMORROW/TO DO LIST:

CREATE YOUR OWN INSPIRING QUOTE AND SHARE YOUR WISDOM WITH OTHERS!

_____

_____

Date ___/___/20__

STRESSFUL MOMENTS:

_____

_____

HAPPY MOMENTS:

_____

_____

Family Bonding Time...

-WRITE OR DRAW SOMETHING SILLY IN THE SPACE DOWN BELOW THAT WILL PUT A HUGE SMILE ON YOUR FACE. ALWAYS TRY TO GO TO BED SMILING AND FEELING HAPPY!

-THINK OF WAYS YOU CAN MAKE YOUR DAY EVEN BETTER TOMORROW.

-ALWAYS SHARE YOUR THOUGHTS AND CONCERNS (even when it is hard to do sometimes) WITH YOUR LOVING FAMILY FOR PROPER GUIDANCE AND GREAT IDEAS. WRITE THEM DOWN BELOW IF NEEDED.

"Some people dream of SUCCESS while others wake up and WORK HARD for it."(2)

~unknown

Date ___ / ___ /20__

STRESSFUL MOMENTS:

_____

_____

_____

HAPPY MOMENTS:

_____

_____

_____

PLAN AHEAD TODAY TO MINIMIZE YOUR STRESS TOMORROW.

(OR YOU CAN JUST WRITE OR DRAW SOMETHING SILLY DOWN BELOW AND GO TO BED SMILING.)

PLANS FOR TOMORROW/TO DO LIST:

CREATE YOUR OWN INSPIRING QUOTE AND SHARE YOUR WISDOM WITH OTHERS!

_____

_____

Date ___/___/20__

STRESSFUL MOMENTS:

_____

_____

HAPPY MOMENTS:

_____

_____

_____

Family Bonding Time...

-WRITE OR DRAW SOMETHING SILLY IN THE SPACE DOWN BELOW THAT WILL PUT A HUGE SMILE ON YOUR FACE. ALWAYS TRY TO GO TO BED SMILING AND FEELING HAPPY!

-THINK OF WAYS YOU CAN MAKE YOUR DAY EVEN BETTER TOMORROW.

-ALWAYS SHARE YOUR THOUGHTS AND CONCERNS (even when it is hard to do sometimes) WITH YOUR LOVING FAMILY FOR PROPER GUIDANCE AND GREAT IDEAS.

WRITE THEM DOWN BELOW IF NEEDED.

"BELIEVE IN YOUR GIFTS: cherish them and explore their possibilities."(2)
~unknown

Date ___/___/20__

STRESSFUL MOMENTS:

_____

_____

_____

HAPPY MOMENTS:

_____

_____

_____

PLAN AHEAD TODAY TO MINIMIZE YOUR STRESS TOMORROW.
(OR YOU CAN JUST WRITE OR DRAW SOMETHING SILLY DOWN BELOW AND GO TO BED SMILING.)
PLANS FOR TOMORROW/TO DO LIST:

CREATE YOUR **OWN** INSPIRING **QUOTE** AND **SHARE YOUR WISDOM** WITH OTHERS!

_____

_____

Date ___/___/20__

STRESSFUL MOMENTS:

_____

_____

HAPPY MOMENTS:

_____

_____

Family Bonding Time...

-**WRITE OR DRAW SOMETHING SILLY IN THE SPACE DOWN BELOW THAT** WILL PUT A HUGE SMILE ON YOUR FACE. ALWAYS TRY TO GO TO BED SMILING AND FEELING HAPPY!

-**THINK** OF WAYS YOU CAN MAKE YOUR DAY EVEN BETTER TOMORROW.

-**ALWAYS SHARE** YOUR THOUGHTS AND CONCERNS (even when it is hard to do sometimes) WITH YOUR LOVING FAMILY FOR PROPER GUIDANCE AND GREAT IDEAS. WRITE THEM DOWN BELOW IF NEEDED.

"BE BRAVE AND WILD AT HEART: make mistakes and don't be afraid to ask questions. Embrace all the things that make you unique."(2)   ~unknown

Date ___/___/20__

STRESSFUL MOMENTS:

_____

_____

_____

HAPPY MOMENTS:

_____

_____

_____

PLAN AHEAD TODAY TO MINIMIZE YOUR STRESS TOMORROW.
(OR YOU CAN JUST WRITE OR DRAW SOMETHING SILLY DOWN BELOW AND GO TO BED SMILING.)
PLANS FOR TOMORROW/TO DO LIST:

CREATE YOUR OWN INSPIRING QUOTE AND SHARE YOUR WISDOM WITH OTHERS!

_____

_____

Date ___/___/20__

STRESSFUL MOMENTS:

_____

_____

HAPPY MOMENTS:

_____

_____

Family Bonding Time...

-WRITE OR DRAW SOMETHING SILLY IN THE SPACE DOWN BELOW THAT WILL PUT A HUGE SMILE ON YOUR FACE. ALWAYS TRY TO GO TO BED SMILING AND FEELING HAPPY!

-THINK OF WAYS YOU CAN MAKE YOUR DAY EVEN BETTER TOMORROW.

-ALWAYS SHARE YOUR THOUGHTS AND CONCERNS (even when it is hard to do sometimes) WITH YOUR LOVING FAMILY FOR PROPER GUIDANCE AND GREAT IDEAS. WRITE THEM DOWN BELOW IF NEEDED.

CONGRATS!!! YOU DID IT!!!

You just finished Your Journal! Treat yourself to something nice! Don't forget: *the end is a new beginning!*

We are sure that by now you are in much better control of your emotions and life in general!
We are kindly asking you to **share your results** with people you love and respect.
Also, it would be **much appreciated** if you could give us your feedback and share your experiences with others. We would love to know how The Stress-Less Life Guide changed **YOUR** own life.

And the most important thing:

We want to thank YOU!!! Yes, You and only You!

Without doing your share of the work, the changes in your life and other people's lives wouldn't be possible. With your help, we can improve the quality of life of so many people and helpless animals.

GUESS WHAT?! **THE FUN IS NOT OVER!!!** YOU WILL CONTINUE TO ENJOY YOUR STRESS-LESS AND HAPPY LIFE DURING THE SUMMER OR VACATION TIME!

KEEP PRACTICING IN OUR NEW GUIDE FOR SUMMERTIME OR ANYTIME.

P.S. We are hoping that by now you are holding a new copy of The Stress-Less Life Guide in your hands so you can continue to enjoy your happy and stressless upcoming school or college year!

REFERENCES

1. "Famous Quotes at BrainyQuote." *BrainyQuote*, Xplore,
   www.brainyquote.com/.

2. "Pinterest." *Pinterest*, www.pinterest.com/.

3. Mercola, J. "How Stress Affects Your Body, and Simple Techniques to
   Reduce Stress and Develop Greater Resilience." 10 Apr. 2016.
   https://articles.mercola.com/sites/articles/archive/2016/04/1
   0/how-stress-affects-body.aspx/.

4. "Quotations." *Quotes Wiki*, www.quotes.wiki/.

www.ingramcontent.com/pod-product-compliance
Lightning Source LLC
Chambersburg PA
CBHW081412270326
41931CB00015B/3251